RECOVERING

BIBLICAL SENSUOUSNESS

RECOVERING
BIBLICAL
SENSUOUSNESS

by
WILLIAM E. PHIPPS

THE WESTMINSTER PRESS
Philadelphia

Book Design by Dorothy Alden Smith

Published by The Westminster Press®
Philadelphia, Pennsylvania

PRINTED IN THE UNITED STATES OF AMERICA

Library of Congress Cataloging in Publication Data

Phipps, William E   1930–
  Recovering Biblical sensuousness.

  Includes bibliographical references and index.
  1.   Emotions—Biblical teaching.   2.   Sex and
religion.   3.   Senses and sensation.   I.   Title.
BS680.E4P47   233   75–22348
ISBN 0–664–20805–3

Contents

(Continued on next page)

Part III

Acknowledgments

Grateful acknowledgment is made for permission to quote from the following works:

Sydney Carter, "Lord of the Dance," copyright © 1963 by Galliard Ltd. All Rights Reserved. Used by permission of Galaxy Music Corp., New York, sole U.S. Agent.

W. H. Auden, "For the Time Being: A Christmas Oratorio," *Collected Longer Poems*, copyright © 1969 by W. H. Auden. Used by permission of Random House, Inc.

Copyright material from essays by the author has been reprinted in several chapters in revised or expanded form, and is used by permission of the publishers:

"The Plight of the Song of Songs," *Journal of the American Academy of Religion*, Vol. 42, No. 1 (March 1974).

"Sacramental Sexuality," *Journal of Religion and Health*, Vol. 13, No. 3 (July 1974).

"The Kiss of Love," *Pastoral Psychology*, Vol. 23, No. 221 (Feb. 1972).

"The Sensuousness of *Agape*," *Theology Today*, Vol. 29, No. 4 (Jan. 1973).

Preface

As one who belongs to the Protestant tradition I am dedicated to the principle that the Christian community needs to be continuously reforming. Like John Calvin, I am interested in going behind the immediate past to the more distant past in hope of recovering a former vitality that has been lost. Thus I am a "radical" in the sense in which the term is used in mathematics and in biology. I am *root* oriented and confident that beneficial changes will come by the sprouting forth of new patterns of individual social behavior from the Judeo-Christian roots of our culture.

This book, like my previous ones, is addressed to a wider audience than scholars in the field of religion. Elaborations have been given that would have been superfluous if I were writing merely for those who have an in-depth understanding of our Western cultural history. I resist the aristocratic approach of those specialists who, like Plato, aim at challenging the intelligentsia while believing that the rest are unable to deal critically with their social heritage.

This book is dedicated to my daughter, Anna Catherine, who is developing a *sensible* religion in which the intellect and the senses are integrated as she blossoms in loveliness.

Bill Phipps

Davis and Elkins College
Elkins, West Virginia
Valentine's Day, 1975

Introduction

THE QUAINT TERM "angelism" is occasionally used to diagnose a sickness in Western culture that continues to spread. Philosopher Jacques Maritain, drawing on the medieval definition of "angel" as a bodyless mind, coined the term to refer to the unauthentic human attempt "to play the pure spirit."[1] The scientifically oriented seem to be as susceptible to the illness as the religiously oriented, for both have tried to detach themselves from the corporeal realm. Marshall McLuhan has used the term in reference to our invisible electric milieu: "One of the effects of the speed of light, when you're on the air or on the phone, you no longer have a body. One of the terrifying aspects of the electric revolution is angelism."[2]

The recent space fiction fascination over the ancient invasion of extraterrestrial beings can be related to angelism. Some earthlings fantasize that they are a mutation consisting primarily of intelligence supplied by celestial beings and secondarily of animal trappings provided by primates. Jesus and the Biblical angels fit into this picture as inverted astronauts who made brief visits to our planet, bringing messages from a superior realm above before ascending to their eternal home.

To provide a spatial framework for angelism, contemporary man tenaciously clings to some of the pre-Copernican cosmology. The superlatively good is located *up* in heaven and the bad *down*—on earth or in its underground hell. The baseness of the terrestrial can be discerned at burial services. Embarrassment is often expressed over the presence of kinship that had not been invited—the earth! In an attempt to slur this close relation, plastic grass is used to cover its unsightliness, and the final casting of earth on the casket, in recognition of "dust to dust," is omitted.

The psychology held by those disdainful of the earthly and devoted to the heavenly is a microcosm. The sacred part of man becomes his mind, for that is the part closest to the ethereal sphere of g(o)od. The sensual part below is regarded as the arena for lewd and profane effects of the (d)evil force. Accordingly, studying scriptures and saying prayers—but not sniffing flowers and making love—are classified as religious acts.

Denigration of the physical body is commonplace in the hymns and sermons of pietism. "Ponder nothing earthly-minded," worshipers sing. The angelism of many church people was expressed by William Jennings Bryan at the famous Scopes trial. He proclaimed: "The Christian believes that man came from above. The evolutionist believes he must have come from below."[3]

While the would-be angels, pious and impious, view themselves ever more spiritually or mentally, they are tearing themselves away from their wholesome natural passions. Michael Novak observes:

> Our own civilization in suburban America is probably the most rationalized and "spiritualized" of any in history. We are more thoroughly sundered from biological rhythms, agricultural rhythms, and even the internal rhythms of our own emotions than any people in history. In our lives, mind controls everything possible.[4]

It seems that societies and individuals who accelerate in power tend to decline in feeling. According to psychiatrist Rollo May, three closely related trends appear on the current scene: the separation of reason and emotion, the alienation of person from body, and the use of the body as a machine.[5] Little is being done to bring about *rapprochement* between the cognitive and the affective. Our educational system is unable to correct sensitivity deprivation, for it is devoted to the input of factual information and correlating it with mental constructs. What education is provided for the intimate senses—touch, taste, and smell?

Encounter group therapy has grown rapidly in some places to resensitize atrophied feelings. It concentrates on intimate psychosomatic interaction, although much of its activity is simulated and somewhat artificial. The encounter group has its place in our emotionally starving culture, but it often lacks the resources for lasting rehabilitation. Affection for strangers and steadfast love cannot be turned on like a spigot at a group session.

The dominant conviction expressed in this book is that a recovery of some neglected aspects of Biblical religion can do much to combat the affective impoverishment of modern society and provide us with a holistic view of life. An open-minded and careful reexamination of our Judeo-Christian heritage is needed for the rightful reintegration of the reason-emotion, mind-body, subject-object, and spirit-flesh personality splits.

Contrary to opinions often held, the Bible does not emphasize the otherworldly at the expense of the natural. According to a creation story, "The Lord God formed man *(adam)* of dust from the ground *(adamah).*" The pun here can be preserved in English by saying that *humans* were created from the *humus.* The Genesis writers indicate that man and animals have much in common: both are made by God from the good earth below and are given "the breath of life." (Gen. 1:30; 2:7; 7:15.) The fact that a person is commonly called "flesh" in Jewish Scriptures rather than "spirit" shows that emphasis is placed on the sentient life. Spirit-flesh contrasts refer only to the distinction between God and his creation.[6] In the Bible the verb "to know" pertains both to experiencing sensually and to comprehending mentally. The good person is the humble (from *humus*) person; sensuality is not regarded as the source of sinful conduct.[7]

Archbishop William Temple argued that the Bible presents "the most avowedly materialistic of all the great religions. . . . Its own most central saying is: 'The Word was made flesh,' where the last term was, no doubt, chosen because of its specially materialistic associations."[8] Norman Brown also finds significance in the movement from the abstract to the concrete in nascent Christianity. He rightly sees the gospel as "not an ascent from body to spirit, but the descent of spirit into body: incarnation not sublimation." Consequently the Christian awakens "not from a body but to a body."[9]

Because of misleading translations and twisted expositions, it has been thought that the apostle Paul was an advocate of angelism. The King James Version wrongly represents him as writing about "our vile body," and a host of interpreters presuppose that he advocated a spiritual life unmarred by carnal concerns.[10] Actually, that most influential of all Christian theologians describes man as "out of the earth, earthly" (I Cor. 15:47) and refers to "a spiritual body" *(sōma pneumatikon)* as the ultimate human condition (v. 44). Rudolf Bultmann shows that Paul is not a dualist in his use of the term body *(sōma):* "The *sōma* is not a something that outwardly clings to a man's real self, but belongs to its very essence, so that we can say man does not have a *sōma;* he is *sōma.*"[11] When Paul contrasted those living "in the flesh" with those living "in the Spirit" he was not referring to psychosomatic dualism but was distinguishing between those living at enmity with God and persons reconciled to him.

Thus Biblical religion does not attempt to affirm the supremacy of the spiritual by depreciating the material. Its leaders lived on the boundary where the divine percolates through matter. The stuff of their humanity is essentially neither mind nor body, neither spirit nor flesh. Biblical men and women are represented as having *spirited* bodies. The Latin term *spiritus* means "breath," and is associated with liveliness and energy. The spirit in bodies should not be thought of as a separate substance grafted on to life. Rather, it is a dimension of life itself, making every*body* enthusiastic and sensitive.

The Biblical view of man's place in nature was largely replaced in postapostolic Christianity by a tyranny of the spirit over the flesh. The attention given in church history to the total body is somewhat parallel to its changing role in Baptism. Originally, as the Greek root of "baptism" suggests, the initiation rite of Christians was probably immersion of the body. Later, the sprinkling of a few drops on the cranium virtually replaced the ancient mode. The church's interest in the bodily has diminished like the water of the ritual. There may be some significance in the fact that the circumcision seal for the Israelite covenant pertained to the tender penis whereas in European Christianity the corresponding seal for the Christian covenant involved the hard head. Be that as it may, it is apparent that Christians succumbed to some alien outlooks in believing that the soul housed in the top of the body is essentially separate from the belly and below. Edward Gibbon sums up the result of this polarization:

> Vainly aspiring to imitate the perfection of angels, they [medieval Christians] disdained . . . every earthly and corporeal delight. . . . The unfeeling candidate for heaven was instructed not only to resist the grosser allurements of the taste or smell, but even to shut his ears against the profane harmony of sounds, and to view with indifference the most finished productions of human art.[12]

In general, the joyful and sensuous religion of the Bible became vapid and literally non-sense. The viewpoint of John Milton, who is credited with inventing the term "sensuous" and giving it a favorable connotation, is one of the notable exceptions to this trend. Another is Martin Luther. Friedrich Nietzsche remarked perceptively: "Detractors of the flesh have always abounded among Germans, and perhaps Luther's greatest merit was to have had the courage of his sensuality."[13]

It is my hope that a return to the Biblical perspective of an integrated mindbody will eliminate the persistent angelism disease, and restore vitality to the church. Hence, studies in this book will show in considerable detail that the Bible strongly affirms the goodness of sense experiences and vigorously endorses the wholeness involved in the proper expression of human emotions.

The sequence of chapters has been determined by the Biblical content. Part I describes motifs that are mainly featured in the Old Testament. It explores two expressions of Hebrew holism: dance in general and a song in particular. The ancient Israelites sang about the human body, God's most perfect creation, and honored dance as a lovely disclosure of that body. However, allegorical interpretation in Gentile Christianity has cleverly but dishonestly attempted to erase the references to physical dance and erotic love in the Scriptures. Chapter 1 sketches the history of religion and dance, and focuses on how Semitic culture related the emotion of religion to the motion of the body. Chapter 2 finds in the Song of Songs a profound sensitivity to natural and human beauty, and traces the bewildering interpretive schemes that have been imposed on that book in an effort to defuse its sexual passion.

Part II is centered on the New Testament. It examines important affectional themes not fully treated in my previous books on the humanity of Jesus. Some of his emotions are observed in Chapter 3, and compared with feelings which have been sanctioned in the history of Christianity. In Chapter 4 an attempt is made to relate the symbolism of sexual relations to the sacraments that Jesus instituted. There it will be seen that the incarnation and the imitation of Christ continue to be cardinal doctrines in my theologizing.

Sensuous themes that are equally prominent in the Old and the New Testament are analyzed in Part III. Chapter 5 reexamines the term *agapē*, the basic term for "love" in the Greek Bible. That term is at the heart of both the Israelite Song of Songs and the Christian song of songs in I Cor., ch. 13. A new semantic investigation seriously questions the oft-made allegation that *agapē* is a term virtually coined by Biblical writers to mean antipassionate love. Can intense human affection be seen as a manifestation of Christian love? Chapter 6 surveys Scripture to see how the religious was related to the beautiful, especially as experienced by the intimate senses of smell, taste, and touch. What significance did Biblical men and women find in these often neglected senses? In Chapter 7, the "kiss of love," a particular Biblical expression of the tactile gone religious, is given special consideration. Chapter 8 surveys the speculations about Paradise in the Semitic culture. This eschatology reveals again a close association between religion and simple sense experiences.

A threefold thrust is found in each of the studies that follow. In differing orders these aspects are presented: (1) the sensuousness of some aspect of Biblical religion; (2) the way in which it became desensitized in church history; and (3) some current efforts to resensitize it in the Christian community. The concluding chapter will review these three facets and give special attention to outlining ways in which Christological principle can be related to enfleshment practice.

Throughout the book the Biblical and classical translations are usually the author's own.

1

Dance and Religion

THROUGHOUT WORLD HISTORY, dance and religion have been closely intertwined. In many cultures dancing is the liveliest social activity, affording opportunities for reinforcing ethnic bonds and for celebrating the divine powers. "To Africans," writes Basil Davidson, "the most important art is dancing. Dancing fuses the two central concerns of African life: religion and community relationships."[1] A similar association of dance and religion can be found in the culture of the American Indians and of the many other pretechnological peoples of the globe.[2] Dance was associated with rites of passage—birth, puberty, marriage, death—and with rites of intensification—before battles, in time of drought, and the like.

The Japanese sacred dance, *kagura*, is as old as the culture in which it is embedded. It is traced to a mythical origin: the mirth goddess dances to lure the sun goddess from a cave and thus bring light to the world. At Shinto shrines this myth is reenacted. Japanese Buddhism incorporated dance into some of its ceremonies.[3]

In the ancient strata of the religions of India, dance is also prominent. The gods are represented in the Vedas as participating in a dance of creation.[4] Shiva, the divine dancer par excellence, throughout the long history of Hinduism, has personified the shifting cosmic energy that creates, preserves, and destroys.[5] In Hinduism, dancing by humans is a worshipful imitation of that divine activity which generated the world.

Inspired dances were performed in the mystery cults of Greece,

and classical drama arose from them.[6] A description of the outstanding Bacchic cult is provided by two playwrights of the Periclean era.
Aristophanes composed this invocation to Dionysus:

> Come with wild and saucy paces
> Mingling in our joyous dance,
> Pure and holy, which embraces
> All the charms of all the Graces.[7]

Euripides has Dionysus assert: "I ordained dances and established my
rites, that I might manifest my godhead to men."[8] That dramatist
portrays the frenzy stimulated by flute and drum as the *sine qua non*
of worship in the mysteries. For him and others in his culture poetry,
music, and dance were inseparable. They thought of the "chorus"
(choros) as basic to their theater and recognized that *choros* meant
"round dance with song."[9] The vases, statues, and other extant art
works of the ancient Greeks often display the beauty of their choral
dances.[10]

Apropos of this sampling of dance in world religions are the reflec-
tions of philosopher Friedrich Nietzsche and theologian Gerardus
van der Leeuw. The former expresses a characteristic outlook of
ancient charismatic leaders when his Zarathustra speaks thus: "Now
a god dances through me."[11] Van der Leeuw holds that dance "is the
oldest, and to a certain extent the most elementary religious art." He
states the universality of dance in a mythical manner: "God moved,
and he set us upon this earth in motion. . . . Man dances because he
is freed, mobilized by a moving power."[12]

Dance seems to have developed along these lines: communal religion that articulates peak experiences was the mother of dance, which
in turn produced song.[13] The coupling of somatic-based dance with
psychic-based lyrics produced a total art "in which man uses all his
functions, his soul and his body, his Logos and his rhythm, in which
he not only plays, speaks, and sings, but also acts, performs."[14]

DANCE IN THE BIBLICAL ERA

The Bible indicates that dancing had reached a complex stage of
development among the Israelites. Although the Hebrew language is

not noted for its rich variety of vocabulary, it nevertheless has some ten verb roots for describing the nuances of choreography.[15] This shows that much attention was given to dance movements. Unlike some other religions, the Hebrews seem to have associated the dance only with occasions of gladness. In several places their Scriptures describe the mood of dance as the opposite of that of mourning (Ps. 30:11; Lam. 5:15; Eccl. 3:4; Jer. 31:13). It was usually a group rather than a solo performance.

One type of dance was the victory celebration in which women participated. The deliverance from Pharaoh's cavalry stimulated this response: "Miriam the prophetess, the sister of Aaron, took a tambourine in her hand; and all the women followed her, dancing to the sound of tambourines" (Ex. 15:20).[16] In a similar manner Jephthah's daughter rejoiced over the return of her victorious father (Judg. 11:34) and the Israelite women celebrated the heroic deeds of David (I Sam. 18:6–7). On each occasion a simple tom-tom-like instrument of stretched animal skin was beaten with the hand to provide a pulsating rhythm.

The annual Hebrew festivals were also occasions for folk dancing. For example, a vintage harvest celebration at Shiloh featured dancing girls. During the history of Israel the vineyard dance increased in popularity, for ancient sources indicate that it was celebrated two or three times each year.[17] Even though translations disguise the fact, dancing was also commonplace at the other festivals. The Hebrew term *hag*, usually rendered "feast" or "festival" in English Bibles, originally meant "a round dance." Only once is the term translated "dance" in the King James Version (I Sam. 30:16). Yet, on the basis of the etymology of *hag*, Emil Hirsch asserts that "the religious dance constituted the principal feature of every festival."[18] Also, the Hebrew terms that are usually translated as "joy" or "gladness" are connected with cultic dancing.[19]

Glimpses of the procession associated with Israelite worship show it to have been more like a boisterous Israeli hora than a solemn march.[20] W. O. E. Oesterley and other scholars plausibly suggest that a verse from Ps. 118 may be translated: "Join the sacred dance in a single file around the horns of the altar."[21] Another psalm helps us visualize the way the encircling dance took place: "Singers lead;

minstrels come last; in the middle girls play on tambourines" (Ps. 68:25). From this description Louis Epstein concludes that among the Israelites there was no objection to the mixing of sexes in dancing as there was later in medieval Judaism.[22] The psalmists' instructions blend with Isaiah's comment on the exuberant way his countrymen worshiped: "For you there shall be songs as on a festival night and gladness of heart as when one moves with music to the hill of the Lord" (Isa. 30:29).

On the basis of these passages and others, W. Robertson Smith has observed that Hebrew religion was predominantly full of mirth. "Hilarity prevailed," he claims; "men ate, drank and were merry together, rejoicing before their God."[23] Hebrew worship was something more to be danced with the body than cogitated by the mind. J. Millar has rightly suggested: "It found its proper aesthetic expression in a merry sacrificial feast. . . . To such a religion dancing would be a natural adjunct. The cultus was not a system of rites, artifically contrived to express and maintain theological doctrines, but the free outcome of religious feelings."[24] It is thus understandable that Eli, a priest at the Shiloh tabernacle, had difficulty judging whether Hannah was moved by the Spirit or under the influence of alcoholic spirits (I Sam. 1:13–15).

W. O. E. Oesterley argues that dancing was such a customary part of the Hebrew cultus that writers often took it for granted and overlooked calling attention to it. He states:

> The Mosaic legislation makes no provision for the posture to be assumed in the presence of the deity, nor does it say anything about singing in worship; but it is difficult to believe that there were not fixed modes in regard to these which have been in vogue from time immemorial; and therefore they needed no mention. The same may be postulated in the case of the sacred dance. . . . In those passages in the Old Testament in which religious dancing is recorded there is no hint of disapproval, let alone prohibition. It is therefore evident that it must have been looked upon as a usual and integral part of worship.[25]

Some Israelites participated in song and dance in order to facilitate religious ecstasy. Samuel informed Saul at Gibeah that he would "be turned into another man" after joining "a band of prophets coming down from a hill-shrine, led by harp, tambourine, flute, and lyre, and filled with prophetic rapture" (I Sam. 10:5–6). J. Lindblom has noted:

> Dancing is not directly mentioned in connection with Israelite prophets. But when we recall . . . the importance of dancing in the Israelite cult, we are entitled to assume that the primitive prophets also used dancing to evoke ecstasy. It is very likely that the prophets in Gibeah came dancing from the high places to the tones of rhythmic music.[26]

In a similar manner Sigmund Mowinckel describes the role of dance in Israelite worship: "The dance is a spontaneous human expression of the sense of rapture, and hence it is regarded and utilized as a means to bring about this rapture and an experience of holy powers and the presence of the divine."[27]

Alfred Guillaume and others have posited that the Israelite prophetic band was similar to the dervish orders that have for many centuries been found in Islamic culture. Both Semitic groups have employed a whirling dance accompanied by tambourines and other musical instruments to propel them into mystic orbit. In both there is "a deep stirring of the emotions consciously directed towards the losing of self in the contemplation of God."[28] The last and climactic Hebrew psalm—which calls on string, wood, and brass instrumentalists to provide hallelujah music for dancing—would have been especially appropriate for the ecstatic dervishes.

The most outstanding dancer in Israel's history was King David. He "danced before the Lord with all his might" when the Ark was brought into Jerusalem. On that occasion he wore the official garment of the priests, the linen ephod, which suggests that the sacred dance was accepted by the priesthood as well as by the prophets of Israel. Intoxicated by horns blowing, cymbals clashing, and other music, he threw his body about with great abandon. Indeed, four different Hebrew words are used to describe his gyrations. One term, *raqad*, is used elsewhere with reference to uninhibited lambs frolicking and children skipping (I Chron. 15:29; Ps. 114:4; Job 21:11). The combination of *pazaz* and *karar* refer to a leaping and rotating movement that still characterizes synagogue dancing in Israel.[29] The fourth term, *saḥaq*, which has also the broader connotation of "to be jubilant," is elsewhere used to describe playful conduct (II Sam. 6:5, 21; Prov. 8:30–31).

The ancient Israelites did not unconditionally approve of every kind of dance. They rejected some of the dance conduct associated with the indigenous people of the land where they had settled. The Canaanites engaged in an orgiastic dance that was deemed morally objectionable because it was associated with self-mutilation and cult prostitution. In the story of Elijah's contest on Mt. Carmel, it is said that his adversaries worshiped Baal in this frenzied manner: "They cried aloud and gashed themselves with swords and spears, as was their custom, until the blood ran" (I Kings 18:28). This description harmonizes with the extrabiblical accounts of the Canaanite sacred dance in honor of Baal Marqad, "the Lord of dance."[30] The ancient writer Apuleius gives the most graphic account of this dance by priests of the same culture some centuries later:

> They went forth . . . shouting and dancing, like mad persons, to the sound of the pipe. . . . They would bend down their necks, and spin around so that their hair flew out at a circle; they would bite their own flesh; finally, everyone took his two-edged weapon and wounded his arms.[31]

This self-lacerating type of conduct was prohibited by Israelite law, and recorded instances of its violation are uncommon (Deut. 14:1; Jer. 41:5; cf. Zech. 13:6)

The Israelites also rejected the wanton characteristic of the Canaanite sacred dance. The Canaanites copulated at their shrines in imitation of the practices of their gods. According to their mythology, the fertility of fields, herds, and humans was dependent on Baal's sexual union with his sister Anath. A Ras Shamra text describes the annual encounter in this manner:

> Baal beholds the maiden Anath . . . he seizes and holds her womb;
> She seizes and holds his stones . . . to conceive and bear. . . .
> Calves the cows drop: an ox for maiden Anath. . . .
> Our progenitor is eternal, to all generations our begetter.[32]

In the Palestinian countryside there were a number of "high places" equipped with cult objects called Asherahs, probably phallic in appearance, where the alleged sexual actions of divine powers were simulated. The female role of Anath (designated as Ashtaroth in the Bible) was performed by "holy" whores, while the male participants acted like Baal. To worship was to "go a whoring" (Hos. 4:12; Ps. 106:39; KJV), inasmuch as sexual expression was unrestrained at those fertility rites. Amos probably had this cult practice in mind when he made this charge: "Father and son go to the prostitute, profaning my holy name" (Amos 2:7). Also, the "golden calf" episode may reflect the antipathy of the Israelite religious establishment toward the sexual excesses associated with the Canaanite sacred dance.

But neither dance nor sexuality was inherently defiling in the Hebrew religion. Sexuality was Yahweh's good handiwork and the sanctions of his covenant with his people were to control the ways in which it was expressed. The Israelite prophets judged promiscuous sex at shrines to be both sacrilegious and useless.[33] Accordingly, dancing at Israelite places of worship was expected to be chaste. The criticism of licentious dancing in the golden calf story should not be interpreted as a condemnation of dance per se, for the same term *(mahol)* used for dance in that story is also used in The Psalms to refer to a fitting mode for praising Yahweh (Ex. 32:19; Ps. 149:3; 150:4).

In the first century of the Christian era, song and dance continued to have a prominent place in the Jewish culture. The Levitical musicians—who, according to Scripture, were selected to "prophesy with lyres, harps, and cymbals" (I Chron. 25:1)—were still functioning in the Herodian temple. The Mishnah describes the exuberant dance that climaxed the Tabernacles festival: "Pious men danced with torches in their hands and sang songs of joy while the Levites played on harps, lyres, cymbals, trumpets, and other musical instruments on the fifteen steps leading down from the Court of the Israelites to the Court of Women." It was said of the gala occasion: "The man who has never seen the joy of the night of this feast has never seen real joy in all his life."[34] During the fiesta, which lasted through the nights of one week, Rabbi Simeon ben Gamaliel celebrated by dancing and flinging eight torches into the air one after another and catching each of them![35]

Appreciation of dancing has continued unabated in medieval and modern Judaism. A fifth-century Christian bishop tried to rid Alexandria of its Jews, in part because of their "fondness for dancing" on the Sabbath.[36] Israel Abrahams states: "By far the most popular athletic amusement of the Jews in the Middle Ages was the dance. . . .Gesticulations, violent leaps and bounds, hopping in a circle, rather than graceful pose or soft rhythmic movements, characterized the Jewish dances both of ancient and medieval times."[37] The way in which dance was integrated into the worship of some Jewish sects has been summarized thus:

> The Kabbalists of the city of Safed went over the hills of Galilee to welcome the mystic Queen Sabbath with the singing of psalms and dancing. . . . The Hasidim danced on Friday night around the rabbi's banquet table. . . . In the Yemenite Jewish communities the Sabbath welcoming dances were danced on tiptoe with vibrations, in ankles and kneejoints, the dancers working themselves up to religious ecstasy. Israel Baal Shem Tov . . . taught his followers that "the dances of the Jews before his Creator are prayers" and quoted the Psalmist, "All my bones shall say: 'Lord, who is like unto Thee?' " (Psalms 35:10.)[38]

According to St. Benedict, *laborare est orare* ("to work is to pray"). But Hasidim founder Besht might well have said, *saltare est orare* ("to dance is to pray").

Jesus showed himself to be a true son of Israel by blending the solemn with the festive. His life-style was in accord with an Israelite sage's observation that there is "a time to weep, and a time to laugh; a time to mourn, and a time to dance" (Eccl. 3:4). Jesus contrasted the outlook of his band to that of others, who were like quarreling children who refuse to dance (Luke 7:31–34). On another occasion, when his followers were criticized for not fasting regularly as the disciples of John the Baptist did, he compared his way of life to a wedding party (Luke 5:33–34), where merry songs and dances would have been the usual mode of celebration.[39]

Jesus held that rhythmic bodily expressions of joy were not only appropriate when circumstances were delightful but also when confronting personal opposition. Those who are rejected because of their identification with him are advised to "be glad and dance for joy" (Luke 6:23). Perhaps Jesus realized that the self-abandonment of enthusiastic dancing was a graphic way of illustrating his paradox that becoming lost in devotion is the avenue to self-fulfillment (Luke 9:24–25).

The joyful life-style advocated by Jesus is reinforced by his picture of the sullen behavior of those who reject it. The parable of the lost sons, his most perfect teaching with respect to divine-human relationships, has a tragic ending. The sulky elder brother, who represents the unforgiving and calculating member of the religious establishment, is unwilling to join in the "music and dance" feast given in honor of the repentent prodigal (Luke 15:25).

The original languages of early Christianity suggest more dancing in the life of Jesus than translators convey. We know that Jesus taught in Aramaic and that he probably used the Semitic root *duts* which refers to dancing.[40] If the Aramaic word for "dance" is behind the verb "rejoice" in Luke 10:21, then Jesus danced for joy after his disciples returned from a successful mission. Also, a processional dance may well have greeted Jesus as he entered Jerusalem at the time we now celebrate as Palm Sunday. The Mishnah informs us that during that era it was customary at one festival to carry palm branches to the Temple and sing from Ps. 118:25: "Hosanna! . . . O Lord, give us success."[41] According to standard English translations, Luke describes Jesus' descent of the Mount of Olives thus: "The whole multitude of the disciples began to rejoice *(chairein)* and praise God with a loud voice." The Greek word here translated "rejoice" is used in Ps. 30:11 to translate the main Semitic term for dance *(maḥol)*. Also, the Greeks assumed that their word for dance, *choros*, was derived from *chara*, the substantive form of *chairein*.[42] Hence it is likely that there was dancing on that Palm Sunday when the Passover pilgrims shouted, "Hosanna to the Son of David!" They may have been remembering King David's dancing as he once approached Jerusalem.

Jesus may have led his disciples in a sacred dance on the night before his crucifixion. The Gospels suggest that they participated in a Passover celebration that was concluded on a musical note.[43] The Mishnah states that several Hallel psalms (Ps. 115–118) were customarily sung after the Passover meal.[44] Those psalms conclude, as we have seen, with an exhortation to join in a processional circle dance. The Acts of John, which dates from the second or third century, elaborates on that episode in the upper room at Jerusalem:

> Before he was arrested . . . he assembled us all and said, "Before I am delivered to them, let us sing a hymn to the Father. . . . So he told us to form a circle, holding one another's hands. . . . He began to sing the hymn and sang, "Glory be to thee, Father." And we circled round him and answered him, "Amen." . . . "He who does not dance does not know what happens." "Amen." "If you follow my dance, see yourself in me." . . . After the Lord had so danced with us, my beloved, he went out.[45]

That noncanonical representation of Jesus as a dance leader fits well with the Fourth Gospel's portrayal of Jesus. In the upper room he encouraged his disciples to be cheerful and share in his joy (*chara;* John 15:11; 16:33). Also, in the prologue of that Gospel, Jesus is presented as the bodily expression of divine Wisdom *(logos).* Wisdom is personified in Scripture as a dancer who gave delight to God:

> I was his darling day after day,
> Dancing in his presence continually,
> Dancing here and there over his world.
> (Prov. 8:30–31)

These depictions of Jesus also harmonize with Zephaniah's eschatological oracle. That prophet boldly envisaged the Lord as dancing victoriously in the midst of Jerusalem:

> He will exult with joy over you,
> he will renew you by his love;
> he will dance with shouts of joy for you
> as on a day of festival.
> (Zeph. 3:17, Jerusalem Bible)[46]

Unlike the Gospels, the letters of the New Testament do not refer to dancing. Although the apostle Paul did not explicitly relate religion to dance, his interpretation of Christianity suggests several correlations. He was aware of the classical meaning of the term *charis*, "grace" (Col. 4:6), and from that meaning he developed his distinctive theological concept. *Charis* had earlier been used to mean beauty of expression that gives delight.[47] The artistic dancer was then, as now, one who had so mastered the exacting techniques of the art that he or she could not only perform the routine in a pleasing way but also improvise with ease. In an analogous manner, Paul believed that the life-style acceptable to God contains both strenuous effort and a freedom of form. From his own experiences he realized that devotion to the commandments of Judaism afforded an unsatisfying religious experience. Only when he received grace—a spontaneity in life resulting from guilt release—did he find fulfillment. In retrospect he viewed the mastery of legal requirements during his maturation as a preparation for internalizing the graciousness of God.

The concept of "transformation" *(metamorphōsis)*, which Paul used in reference to the Christian's experience, also has dance associations. In Romans he appealed to Christians to present their bodies to God and to become metamorphosed (Rom. 12:1–2; cp. II Cor. 3:18). The ecstatic dance is an excellent symbol of that radical personal change. It graphically depicts the Christian's emancipation from the cocoon of dreary routine which weighs down his spirit and thwarts self-transcendence.

Theologian Harvey Cox has recognized that "dance both uses the body to celebrate and also celebrates the body." Both of these functions can be related to Paul's concerns, for he held that the body was an honorable part of the total personality. After pointing out that the Christian's temple is his psychophysical self and not an external shrine, the apostle exhorts: "Praise God in your body" (I Cor. 6:20). Those words, written with regard to sexual morality, were a response to some Gnostic-prone Christians who did not realize that the celebration of God involves more than cerebrating. Paul recognized how difficult it is to express our emotions and acknowledged that communication with God is sometimes nonverbal. "We . . . groan inwardly," he wrote, "as we wait for . . . the liberation of our bodies. . . . We do not know how to pray as we ought, but the Spirit himself intercedes for us with sighs too deep for words" (Rom. 8:23, 26). Cox aptly comments: "Some who cannot say a prayer may still be able to dance it."[48]

Paul advised Christians to "be filled with the Spirit" by participating in musical rhythms (Eph. 5:18–19; Col. 3:16). Although he did not single out the sacred dance as a way of worship, it was, as we have seen, usually associated with singing in his Jewish culture. Moreover, missionary Paul was writing to people saturated with the Greek culture, which included dance in practically all its religious rituals. Lillian Lawler writes: "The Greek almost never sang or chanted verse without using an accompanying movement of some part of his body."[49]

DANCE IN CHURCH HISTORY

The Greek fathers of the early church were more appreciative of religious dancing than were the Latin fathers. The Greek cultural inheritance helps to explain this difference in viewpoint. Lucian of Samosata, writing in the second century A.D. about the Greeks, claimed that "not a single ancient mystery cult can be found that is without dancing."[50]

Greek Christians writing in the third century refer to sacred dancing. Clement of Alexandria was the first to describe Christian worship in which torch-light choral dancing was a significant feature.[51] Hippolytus conceived of Jesus as the "leader of the sacred dance" who directs the movements of his church.[52]

A century later some Greek bishops continued to endorse religious dancing, although they were cautious to distinguish it from unacceptable licentious dancing. Gregory of Constantinople wrote this criticism to Emperor Julian:

> If you are fond of dancing at festivals, then dance as much as you like, but not the shameless dance of the daughter of Herod which accompanied the execution of the Baptist. Rather perform the dance of David before the ark, which I consider to be the approach to God, the swift encircling steps in the manner of the mysteries.[53]

These remarks show that both the pagan mysteries and Biblical customs influenced dancing in the Gentile church. Gregory of Nyssa also had King David as his model for sacred dancing—David, who "by rhythmic bodily movement showed in public his inner state of soul."[54]

John Chrysostom was ambivalent toward dance. Some of his sermons show that he approved of dancing and joined with other bishops in commemorative dances.[55] Yet in other sermons he protests against dancing, claiming that "where there is dancing there is the devil."[56] He questions: "Who is to dance? No one, for what need is there of dancing? In the Grecian mysteries there are dancings, but in ours, silence and decency, modesty and bashfulness."[57]

Eusebius recorded that the triumph of Constantine the Great caused much jubilation among Christians: "They danced and sang in city and country alike, giving honor first of all to God."[58] That fourth-century historian pointed out that Christians in his day engaged in the same type of worship as had been engaged in by a sect in Egypt called the Therapeutae.[59] Philo, a contemporary of Jesus, described that Hellenistic Jewish community as having a feast in which they ate a meal featuring unleavened bread, sang psalms and imitated the dance of Miriam. Some of the details of that gala ceremony follow:

> They celebrate the sacred festival during the whole night . . . moving their hands and dancing in corresponding harmony, and uttering in an inspired manner songs of thanksgiving. . . . Then, when each chorus of the men and women has feasted separately by itself, like persons in the bacchanalian revels, drinking the pure wine of the love of God, they join together, and the two become one chorus.[60]

Theodoret, another church historian, stated that Christians "danced not only in the churches and the chapels of the martyrs, but also in the theaters, proclaiming the victory of the cross."[61] Dancing such as this was literally both sacred and profane (from *pro fanum*, "before the temple"), because it was done both inside and outside of shrines.

In his careful study *Religious Dances*, E. Louis Backman gives this summary of the dances that were a part of the early Christian lifestyle:

The dances were mostly choral dances and ring-dances, probably always to the accompaniment of hymn singing and psalms. . . . Romping dances also occurred, sometimes hopping and leaping and also gyrating. All the dances appear to have been led by a rhythmic clapping of the hands, which was probably only intermittent, and by stamping of the feet.[62]

Thus the documents of the early Greek Christians provide ample evidence that their worship was more than solemn praying and chanting: it occasionally involved both mild or wild dancing to express gratitude for the "life which is life indeed," which Jesus had brought to fruition. They thought of themselves as fulfilling what Ezekiel proclaimed: "Thus says the Lord God, 'Clap your hands, and stamp your feet'" (Ezek. 6:11).[63]

Although many Greek values were adopted by the Romans, this was not the case with respect to dance. Lincoln Kirstein states: "Dance, as the Greeks understood it, and to a great extent as we understand it, held little meaning for Romans."[64] Curt Sachs, another authority on the history of dance, characterizes the Romans as sober people who participated little in enthusiastic dances, even though many appreciated pantomime.[65] Early in their history dancing was deemed disgraceful: Scipio the Younger, who governed during the era of the Republic, forced the dancing schools to close.[66] Cicero held that no respectable person would dance. He quipped: "Almost no man dances when sober—except perhaps a lunatic."[67] It was also considered improper for ladies to dance. Russell M. Hughes states of Rome during the Empire period: "Only the paid woman danced; and 'dancer' became a synonym for 'harlot.'"[68]

Latin Christianity divorced dance from song, regarding the latter as the innocent party because it did not greatly stir up the body. This outlook was taken over from Stoicism, the most popular ethical philosophy in Roman culture. It held that the expression of visceral emotions was a vice, while unruffledness *(ataraxia)* and passionlessness *(apatheia)* were the supreme virtues. Accordingly, dancing was regarded as morally suspect, if not outright immoral.

Church architecture was probably another reason why only song was retained. When Christians began to construct churches in the fourth century, they used the basilica as their model. That oblong structure with a raised platform at one end had been designed by the Romans to function as a court of law. Attorneys could there make speeches to juries and politicians could harangue audiences. When the basic basilica design was adopted by Christians, they unwittingly transformed active participants into passive audiences. The earliest record of Christian worship shows that each person was expected to take an active part (I Cor. 14:26), but the basilica church encouraged more mouth movement by preachers and less body movement by congregations. Had there been Roman dance halls and had the Christians used such halls for the architectural design of their sanctuaries, the clergy would have tended to cast themselves more in the role of choreographer than in the role of pulpit orator.

In the fourth century the eloquent orator Ambrose admonished mothers to teach daughters "religion, not dancing." "What modesty can there be," he questioned, "where there is dancing and noise and clapping of hands?" Bishop Ambrose appealed to Cicero's censure of dancing and blended it with a moral wrested from the New Testament:

> Now if, according to the wisdom of this world, either drunkenness or madness is the cause of dancing, what a warning is given to us among the instances mentioned in the divine Scriptures, where John . . . being beheaded at the wish of a dancer, is an instance that the allurements of dancing did more harm than the madness of sacrilegious anger.[69]

Ambrose was troubled by one of Jesus' comments on the improper conduct of fellow humans: "They are like children sitting in the market place and calling to one another, 'We piped to you, and you did not dance' " (Luke 7:32). The bishop used the literary device of allegory to remove the literal implication of those words. Jesus was criticizing, he claimed, not those who reject pleasurable dancing but those who do not strive for Christian purposes. He elaborated further:

> Paul danced spiritually, when for us he stretched forward, and forgetting the things which were behind, and aiming at those which were before, he pressed on to the prize of Christ. And you, too, when you come to baptism, are warned to raise the hands, and to cause your feet wherewith you ascend to things eternal to be

swifter. This dancing accompanies faith, and is the companion of grace.[70]

Because of the stimulus of Ambrose's sermons, Augustine came to have a fresh interest in Christianity. He acknowledged that the Bishop of Milan taught him the allegorical method for interpreting "things which, taken literally, seemed to teach perversity."[71] Augustine frequently used his clever mind to convert into pious sentiments those Biblical statements which were not in accord with his own preconceived ideas of Christian doctrine. For example, the references in the psalms to worshiping with "timbrel and dance" were interpreted to mean something altogether different from the literal connotation. The skin stretched over the wooden timbrel frame represents the crucifixion of the Christian's physical desires. "Stretch yourself out on the wood," Augustine exhorted, "and be dried from the lust of the flesh." His ignorance of Greek and Hebrew may have contributed to his failure to acknowledge that the last two psalms explicitly commend dancing. This is his exposition of Ps. 149:3: " 'Let them praise His Name in *chorus.*' What does *chorus* mean? . . . Since we are here in a town, almost all know. A *chorus* is a group of singers. To sing in *chorus* means to sing in concord." Actually the Latin term *chorus* had dance associations and the term used by the psalmist *(maholah)* and by the Septuagint translator *(choros)* doubtless referred to dance. Augustine even had reservations about singing psalms, for he believed that this activity was proper only if the worshiper focused on thinking about the words rather than on the pleasure of the music.[72]

Augustine was convinced that dancing was inimical to worship. He said: "Let us rejoice because the martyrs have passed from the world of suffering to the fields of rest; but they have not achieved this by dancing, but by prayer."[73] The Gospel verse, "We piped to you and you did not dance," is interpreted by the Bishop of Hippo in this strange way: "He pipes who commands; he dances who obeys. What else is dancing but following sounds with the motions of the body? . . . In our case dancing means changing our manner of life."[74] This exegetical sleight of hand was offered by Augustine in defense of his abolition of dancing at religious festivals. Regarding the Sabbath, he stated: "It would be better to spend the holy day ploughing than to desecrate it with dancing."[75]

The traditional Latin disdain for dancing, coupled with Augustine's condemnation, resulted in popes and councils outlawing that art throughout the Middle Ages. A gross lack of Biblical knowledge is displayed in the proscriptive edicts, for the ground usually given is that dancing was exclusively originated by the satanic heathen.[76] Religious as well as secular dancing was prohibited. The position of the Western church on dances of all types was summed up in this aphorism: "The devil is the inventor and governor and disposer of dances and dancing."[77] Dom Gougaud has rightly discerned that "there is nothing to prove or even to render it probable that any kind of sacred dance was ever admitted into the liturgy of the church."[78] It is in this light that we should evaluate Jacques Maritain's oft-quoted description of the high mass as "a dance before the ark in slow motion."[79] It is unlikely that the original dancer before the Ark would have found the movement lively enough to be properly defined as "dance."

Ecclesiastical sanctions were not sufficient to eliminate popular dancing. Medieval scholar G. G. Coulton has written:

> It is true that a great deal of dancing went on in the medieval village, just as a good deal of drinking went on. . . . It would be quite impossible, I think, to find any religious writer who admitted the cleric's right to join in any dance whatsoever; and the dance itself is more consistently condemned, even for lay folk, than the tavern.[80]

The carol form, which is now especially associated with Christmas, was developed in the late Middle Ages by traveling minstrels—in spite of the ban on dancing.[81] In Middle English and in French it was called the *carole*, meaning a closed circle dance.[82] The term probably originated with the Greek *choros*, which once referred, as we have seen, to song and dance performers. A French carol in honor of the Christ child that probably goes back to the medieval minstrels has these lines:

> Dance on the right foot,
> Dance on the left foot,

> My good Jesus,
> Dance on both feet.[83]

With the Renaissance came an interest in reviving those art forms which were intrinsic to the classical and Biblical cultures. At that time there were some clergymen who helped to promote secular and religious dancing. In the fifteenth century, Cardinal Pietro Riario staged for the Duke of Milan a pantomime in musical setting that has been called the first ballet.[84] Beginning in the Renaissance and continuing until the present, dances were performed at the Cathedral of Seville by choir boys with castanets before the high altar on festival days.[85] In the *Orchesography*, the outstanding treatment of dance in the sixteenth century, a priest wrote this defense:

> For everyone who has belittled dancing, scores of others have praised and esteemed it. King David danced before the Ark of the Lord and the holy prophet Moses was not angered to see dancing, but grieved that it should take place around a Golden Calf and become an act of idolatry. . . . In the primitive church there was a custom, which has survived into our own times, of dancing and swaying while chanting the hymns of our faith.[86]

In that same century, Bible translator William Tyndale helped to effect a renaissance of the Biblical outlook on dance and religion with this definition: *"Evangelion* (that we call the gospel) is a Greek word; and signifieth good, merry, glad and joyful tidings, that maketh a man's heart glad, and maketh him sing, dance and leap for joy: as when David had killed Goliath the giant, came glad tidings unto the Jews . . . for gladness whereof they sung, danced, and were joyful."[87]

Martin Luther heartily approved of dancing even on Sunday, provided it stayed within the bounds of decency.[88] He pointed out that dances afford excellent occasions for courtship. He was recorded as having said:

> Dances are instituted that courtesy may be learned in company, and friendship and acquaintance be contracted between young men and girls. Here their socializing may be watched, and occasion of honorable meeting given so that having tested a girl we can afterwards let her go about more safely and easily. The Pope formerly condemned dances because he was an enemy of marriage. But let all things be done decently! Let honorable men and ma-

trons be invited to see that everything is proper. I myself would attend dances sometimes, but the youth would whirl less giddily if I did![89]

In his sermon on the feast at Cana, where Jesus helped to supply the drinks for a wedding party, Luther remarked that he and others should not be criticized for dancing and imbibing at parties just because some guests behave immoderately.[90] His own wedding to Katherine was followed by a dance at the town hall.[91]

John Calvin agreed in principle with Luther's Biblical position on dancing, but he did not carry it out in practice. He defended the dance of King David and stated regarding the musical arts: "Pleasure is to be condemned only when it is not combined with reverence for God and not related to the common welfare of society. But music by its nature is adapted to rouse our devotion to God and to aid the well-being of man."[92] However, Calvin lacked Luther's vigor and seems to have been temperamentally too solemn to appreciate dancing. He probably approved of the Geneva ordinance that resulted in the imprisonment of a prominent citizen who committed the indiscretion of "spinning wildly" at a betrothal party.[93] But Percy Scholes, the leading authority on Puritan music, is right in asserting that Calvin condemned the abuse of dancing, not dancing as such.[94] He could not have condemned dancing if he consistently applied his belief that "all things which make for the enriching of this present life are sacred gifts of God."[95]

With respect to dancing, the prominent followers of Calvin do not fit the killjoy caricature drawn by their opponents. In the standards established by Calvinists at the Westminster Assembly in 1647, only "lascivious" dancing is prohibited.[96] Oliver Cromwell threw a great all-night dancing party for his daughter's wedding. One participant described the occasion as having "much mirth with frolics, besides mixt dancing."[97] John Milton, Cromwell's Latin secretary, also loved song and dance. In one of his poems this invitation is extended: "Com, and trip it as ye go / On the light fantastick toe . . ."[98]

> Som times with secure delight
> The up-land Hamlets will invite,
> When the merry Bells ring round,

And the jocond rebecks sound
To many a youth, and many a maid,
Dancing in the Chequer'd shade;
And young and old com forth to play
On a Sunshine Holyday.[99]

John Bunyan would probably have approved of such rustic dancing, for in *Pilgrim's Progress* his liberated prisoners dance after Giant
Despair is slain. That influential allegory continues:

> Now Christiana, if need was, could play upon the viol, and her
> daughter Mercy upon the lute; so since they were so merry dis-
> posed, she played them a lesson, and Ready-to-halt would dance.
> So he took Despondency's daughter, named Much-afraid, by the
> hand, and to dancing they went in the road.[100]

It was during the period of Puritan control of England that John
Playford's book was published entitled *The English Dancing Master:
or Plaine and easie Rules for the Dancing of Country Dances.* That
Puritan churchman's anthology contains dances that have had an
enduring popularity on both sides of the Atlantic.[101]

In seventeenth-century New England there was a guarded acceptance of dance by influential Calvinists. John Cotton found Biblical
precedent for male-female dancing that avoided "wanton dalliances."
Increase Mather probably wrote the tract entitled "An Arrow against
Profane and Promiscuous Dancing, Drawne out of the Quiver of the
Scriptures," but the target of his "arrow" was dancing that stimulates
sexual license. That he did not intend to engage in wholesale condemnation of all dancing is displayed in this judgment: "Dancing or
leaping is a natural expression of joy; so that there is no more sin in
it than in laughter, or any outward expression of inward rejoicing."[102]
The practice of this principle is evidenced in the fact that Timothy
Edwards, Jonathan Edwards' father, in 1694 held a dance in his home
to celebrate his ordination.[103]

During the eighteenth and nineteenth centuries, approval of dancing was withdrawn in most American churches. Margaret Fisk Taylor, in her study of the history of dance in the church, accurately
generalizes: "All conventional Protestant Christians came to assume
that religious dancing might be done by 'primitive savages' or 'be-

nighted pagans,' but never—absolutely never—by Christians."[104]
Only in a few sects noted by the establishment for eccentric behavior
was dancing encouraged. The Shakers believed that worship should
be whole-bodied, as it had been for Miriam and David. One of their
elders explained: "The faculty of dancing . . . was undoubtedly
created for the honor and glory of the Creator. . . . He has created
the hands and the feet, and enabled them to perform their functions.
. . . And shall these important faculties . . . be idle in the service of
God?"[105] Marcus Bach provides this description of the Shakers:

> The dancers . . . were often jubilant as they symbolized with the
> movement of their hands and arms the intaking and outpouring
> of love, or the joy of being washed clean from sin, or the ecstasy
> of getting rid of sin by shaking it out of their bodies until it
> quivered only in the arms, then in the fingers, and was eventually
> absorbed in space.[106]

The purpose of their dancing is also indicated in this Shaker song:

> With ev'ry gift I will unite
> And join in sweet devotion;
> To worship God is my delight,
> With hands and feet in motion.[107]

The Shaker enthusiasm for dancing was carried on by the Mormons. Also a millennialist sect on the American frontier in the early
nineteenth century, the Mormons were waxing in number as the
Shakers began to wane. During the decade when Joseph Smith was
organizing the "Latter-day Saints" in western New York, there was
published in that area, by other millennialists, a book that advocated
the dance for those waiting for the rapturous return of Jesus.[108]
Smith also believed that "dancing has a tendency to invigorate the
spirit and promote health." Consequently, from its pioneering days
onward, the Mormon Church has been the "dancingest denomination" in the United States.[109] Wallace Bennett has written: "As early
as 1854, there were nineteen Church dancing schools in Salt Lake.
All the Church leaders danced. Dancing patterns have kept up with
the times, but all dances are conducted with decorum. . . . Dances
are always opened, and usually closed, with prayer."[110]

In black churches group dancing was prominent, and the ritual was as much African as Christian.[111] The tempo of Afro-American has always evoked a desire to rise and let the whole body be moved by the vibrant syncopation. An eyewitness to a plantation church service recorded this description: "The benches are pushed back . . . and old and young, men and women . . . stand up in the middle of the floor. . . . Sometimes they dance silently, sometimes as they shuffle they sing the chorus of the spiritual. . . . Song and dance are alike extremely energetic."[112]

Nineteenth-century main-line Protestant denominations tended to return to the view the medieval clergy had championed, that all dancing is degrading. This shift seems to have been due in part to the work ethic, which looked on leisure-time activity as a vice, and in part to the abstinence movement. Although the latter was principally directed against intoxicants, the prohibitionists were often zealous to squeeze other sources of merriment out of life.

Methodism was especially critical of dancing, even though it was not considered an evil when the denomination originated. Indeed, in the introduction to John Wesley's *Journal* this personal information is given: "In Worcestershire he occasionally danced with friends and with his sisters almost on every available evening during his visits to Wroot and Epworth."[113] However, in 1872 the General Conference of the Methodist Church declared that dancing was unchristian behavior and that those who refuse to repent of such misconduct should be expelled from the church.[114]

Both folk and ballroom dancing are condemned in a book written in 1869 by a clergyman, J. T. Crane, and prefaced by a Methodist bishop's imprimatur. Entitled *Popular Amusements*, that book is basically medieval in outlook. Cicero's judgment, "No man in his senses will dance," is approvingly quoted along with the saying, "The dancing-master is the devil's drill-sergeant." Crane made these observations: "Nominal Christians may be found at balls and dancing assemblies, but they are persons who have no weight of Christian character. . . . Dancing wastes time, wastes health, scatters serious thought, compromises Christian character, leads to entangling association with frivolous minds and careless hearts."[115]

Other denominations had a similar stultifying outlook on dancing.

A Presbyterian synod in 1860 adopted the position that dancing is "clearly forbidden by the spirit of the gospel" and condemned by the highest Presbyterian judicatory. Church sessions were enjoined to correct the wickedness by excommunicating those who could not be persuaded to change their conduct. During that period Albert Barnes, a Presbyterian minister, wrote: "Dancing, balls, and parties lead to forgetfulness of God. They nourish passion and sensual desire. . . . No child dances into heaven; but many a one dances into hell."

For a sample of nineteenth-century Episcopalian proscription on dancing, remarks by Bishop Meade of Virginia will suffice. Evidently associating the dance with "the world, the flesh, and the devil," he asserted:

> It has always been considered so disreputable to excel in this as a public performer, that such persons have been excluded sometimes from civil, and always from religious privileges, and from respectable society. Can the practice of it, then, even in a more private way, be suitable or becoming in a serious Christian? . . . It is, in itself, wrong, improper, and of bad effect.[116]

James Russell Lowell attacked the values of such churchmen with satirical poetry. He portrayed the bigot of the mid-nineteenth century in this incisive way:

> He who esteems the Virginia reel
> A bait to draw saints from their spiritual weal,
> And regards the quadrille as a far greater knavery
> Than crushing his African children with slavery,
> Since all who take part in a waltz or cotillion
> Are mounted for hell on the Devil's own pillion,
> Who, as every true orthodox Christian well knows,
> Approaches the heart through the door of the toes.[117]

Contemporary Christians, with the exception of some fundamentalists, have generally shed their Victorian corsets. The Methodist Church is typical: their ban on dancing was removed in the post–World War I era. In 1930 the Southern Presbyterian General Assembly officially reversed its earlier condemnation of dancing of every kind by giving positive encouragement to the use of dancing as a wholesome recreation.[118] However, the *Encyclopedia of Southern*

Baptists, apparently expressing the general outlook of the largest denomination in the United States, stated as recently as 1958: "The dance hall has been condemned as 'lascivious and deadly'; and the dance, as fleshly and sinful, a corrupt, corrupting, and gross evil, which, accompanied by immodest dress, close physical contact of the sexes, and lack of restraint 'undermines the morals of our young people.' "[119] The Seventh-Day Adventist Church has also, throughout its history, instructed its members to refrain from dancing, calling it "a school of depravity."[120]

Few churchmen have suggested positive ways for restoring fully the ancient art. Most have scant knowledge of their Judeo-Christian heritage with respect to dance, much less a concern for correcting the historical distortion. This can be illustrated from some basic reference works now used by the two main branches of American Christianity. The article on religious dancing in the *New Catholic Encyclopedia* deals with ways in which many religions have utilized the dance, but no mention is made of the role of dance in Judeo-Christian history. Similarly, Cynthia Pearl Maus's Protestant-oriented anthologies entitled *The Old Testament and the Fine Arts*, *Christ and the Fine Arts*, and *The Church and the Fine Arts* give the impression that the religion of the Bible has no association with the art of dancing.

REUNITING DANCE AND RELIGION

Even though the harsh negative judgment on dance by most Christians in the latter part of the twentieth century has abated, most people have come to view dancing as little more than a social pastime. In ancient cultures the sacred and secular strands of dance were so tightly entwined as to be nondistinguishable, but in modern history the religious aspects of the art have atrophied. The history of dance and religion suggests that peoples in simple cultures have more "soul"-body and self-society integration than highly civilized peoples. If "religion" means being bound together, then the ceremonial dance is a superb mode for uniting an individual with his fellows and with those divine powers that concern him.

Stewart Headlam, a voice crying in the artistic wilderness of Victorian times, made this in-depth observation:

The art of dancing, . . . perhaps more than all other arts, is an outward and visible sign of an inward and spiritual grace . . . [Yet it] has suffered even more than the other arts. . . . Your Manichaean Protestant, and your superfine rationalist, rejects the dance as worldly, frivolous, sensual, and so forth; and your dull, stupid sensualist sees legs, and grunts with satisfaction; but your sacramentalist knows something worth more than both of these. He knows what perhaps the dancer herself may be partially unconscious of, that we live now by faith and not by sight, and that the poetry of dance is the expression of unseen spiritual grace.[121]

Sacred dance researchers have collected a few lyrics composed by those who have dared to put their faith in a dancing Jesus.[122] To provide a sampling of one of the centuries-old poems, two stanzas will be excerpted:

> In a manger laid and wrapp'd I was,
> So very poor, this was my chance,
> Betwixt an ox and a silly poor ass,
> To call my true love to my dance.

> Then up to heaven I did ascend,
> Where now I dwell in sure substance
> On the right hand of God, that man
> May come unto the general dance.[123]

John Wycliffe's band of preachers may have sung this hymn, for he pictured Jesus as one who led the "daunce of love."[124]

In recent years Sydney Carter, an Englishman, has composed the ballad "Lord of the Dance," which also gives a first-person rendition of the life of dance leader Jesus. The lyrics are delightfully combined by Carter with an adaptation of the Shaker tune "Simple Gifts." He has acknowledged that the Shakers were his main inspiration and that he wrote "Lord of the Dance" after witnessing a Shaker dance at a folk festival.[125] During the past decade it has become one of the more popular songs of avant-garde Christianity. Its concluding stanza contains several motifs from the Gospel of John:

> They cut me down and I leap up high—
> I am the life that'll never, never die.
> I'll live in you if you'll live in me—

> I am the Lord of the Dance, said he.
> Dance then wherever you may be.
> .   .   .   .
> And I'll lead you all in the Dance, said he.[126]

In the twentieth century there has been a modest revival of religious dance. The Sacred Dance Guild, formed in 1955, has a membership drawn from a wide variety of religious backgrounds. The most outstanding figure to date is Ted Shawn, who aimed at becoming a clergyman in his youth but decided that he could better perform his "ministry" as an interpretive dancer. He regards the narrow outlooks of congregations and the narrow platforms of sanctuaries as his main hindrances when he attempts to lead worship as a dancer.[127] Also during the past generation Margaret Fisk Taylor has devoted herself to resurrecting worship through symbolic movement. She has directed liturgical dances and has written helpful books on the principles and practice of choreography.[128] She claims that the rhythmic choir has assisted tightly repressed individuals to gain new poise and freedom. By discerning that invocations of praise can come from the movement of hands and legs as well as from the lips, these individuals thereby become totally involved in worship.[129] Doug Adams, drawing on his training in Biblical studies and in dance, has recently written about ways of returning to congregational dancing like that practiced in the early Judeo-Christian tradition so as to make worship throb again.[130] Sister Tina Bernal exemplifies the fact that interpretive dance is also beginning to be appreciated by some contemporary Catholics. Formerly a professional ballerina, she now dances at church altars in her nun's habit in order to celebrate the goodness of the body and to offer it to God.[131]

Happily, there are some who are calling for a more authentic liturgy. In his book *Dancing for God*, Catholic priest Lucien Deiss has commented: "It is sad that Christians do not have the most beautiful and best dances to honor their Lord. . . . The true danger which menaces the Church is not the use of beauty to extol Jesus Christ, but the cluttering of our churches with ugliness and boredom."[132] Protestant John Killinger has also written about the need for reviving sacred dance:

If God cannot be felt in the body, in the entire psychosomatic unity of the person, then he cannot really be said to have an efficacious existence in the life of the person. And the sheer physical restrictions placed upon worshiping congregations in most religious traditions of the last few hundred years have finally done their work and crowded out many people's sensitivity to the divine as belonging to anything more than the intellectual or problem-solving realm of their being. . . . We must relax our extremely repressive attitudes toward the body and begin to use it for what it is, one of the major vehicles we have for communicating and receiving information. Until we do, worship in the fullest dimension will be impossible, and we shall continue to sense something unreal and remote about our liturgies.[133]

Worship forms of the future ought to accentuate more fully that muscles other than those located in the vocal cords are suitable for giving outward expression to inward reverence. The exuberant worshiper does not need "a thousand tongues" to praise God, but he does need his ten toes. Both order and ardor are needed for artistic "speaking in toes," so Paul's wise counsel regarding combining those qualities should be heeded (I Cor., ch. 14). A dancing leg, a praying heart, and a thinking head go well together. Thus a Biblically based liturgy might well contain these lines:

Lift up your heads, hearts, hands, and feet.
We lift them up unto the Lord.

2

The Plight of the Song of Songs

A MEMBER of the postexilic Jewish community wrote down some throbbing sentiments that he had heard sung about a couple in love. That anonymous editor's romantic bent is revealed in the superlative he used in the Hebrew title, *Shir ha-Shirim*, "The Song of Songs," i.e., the loveliest song. He dedicated the work to Solomon, the greatest lover in the Israelite tradition—at least on a quantitative scale!

The Song of Songs is about intimate love. The editor probably contributed little to either the content or the organization of his collection. As if stringing a necklace, he loosely put together folk lyrics of varying lengths expressing different facets of beauty on a unifying theme. He alternated the male and female voices but showed little concern for the sequence of ideas in arranging the stanzas.

The editor no doubt thought the meaning of his anthology would be transparently clear to readers. Even in his own day similar poems of this genre were commonplace in the Near East from Egypt to Mesopotamia.[1] What can be more universally understood than love's old sweet song? If John Milton is correct in his observation that simplicity and sensuousness are the basic ingredients of poetry in any language,[2] the Song of Songs should not have caused problems of interpretation.

It is a prank of history that a poem so obviously about hungry passion has caused so much perplexity and has provoked such a plethora of bizarre interpretations. Even contemporary scholars appear baffled by the Song of Songs. For example, Theophile J. Meek begins his commentary with this amazing and forbidding note: "Of all the books of the Old Testament none is so difficult to interpret."[3] During the past century some scholars claimed to have found in the Song of Songs ritual chants used to simulate the annual springtime marriage of a fertility god and goddess. But in the Hebrew culture, sex had been demythologized: it was considered a proper sphere for man but not for deity. Others found in the Song a script for a theater production, complete with the chorus characteristic of Greek drama. Accordingly, a triangle was worked out, with a villainous Solomon and a virtuous shepherd vying for a rustic damsel. However, it takes much reading between the lines to find this plot, and there are no parallel extra-Biblical dramas of the ancient Near East that might give such a conjecture plausibility.

Several clues in ancient Jewish literature suggest that the Song of Songs was originally a repertoire containing songs for members of wedding parties. First, we know that nuptial feasts lasted for several days[4] and that, for bride and groom, role-playing as royalty was customary during that time. The Mishnah indicates that prior to the Roman destruction of Jerusalem the bridegroom wore a crown,[5] possibly in imitation of King Solomon, who was famous for attracting both wealth and women. Also, as Jeremiah shows, weddings were associated with mirthful music: "The voice of the bridegroom, the voice of the bride, the voices of those who sing" (Jer. 33:11).

It would be anachronistic to interpret the Song of Songs as representing the infatuations and sexual experimentation of promiscuous youth. In the traditional Semitic culture, marriage was covenanted near the age of puberty and intimate male-female association was not sanctioned prior to marriage. That the Song focuses on the betrothed or married couple is made explicit by the term *kallah,* which means "spouse" and is frequently used in reference to the female partner (S. of Songs 4:8 to 5:1; cp. Gen. 11:31; 38:11). Coupled often with that term is *ahoth,* which literally means "sister." In the context of the Song it connotes psychophysical closeness rather than kinship. The idiom "my sister, my bride" could well be rendered "my dear wife."[6]

The sexual innocence of the girl is frequently alluded to by the tower and garden images. Parts of her body are compared to a high fortress that is able to withstand all who might try to destroy its defenses (chs. 4:4; 7:4; 8:10). Previously inaccessible to all men, she now gladly opens up her virginal femininity to the great conqueror, her spouse. He commends her for having been "a garden locked, a fountain sealed" (ch. 4:12) and confesses that he has been looking forward to exploring the lush growth she has cultivated (ch. 7:8).

As lyrics for wedding celebrations in lovely out-of-doors settings, the Song of Songs fits well into the Hebrew religious outlook. In that culture, unlike our own, it was not the unattached who were extolled by song. The first love song of the Bible depicts Adam rapturously exclaiming to his bride: "This at last is bone of my bones, and flesh of my flesh." In that garden story, as in the Song of Songs, woman is of intrinsic value and no mention is made of her fecundity. Also, the sentiments of the couple in the Song who are "intoxicated with love" (ch. 5:1) are echoed in a poem from the book of Proverbs:

> Be grateful for your own fountain,
> And have your pleasure with the wife of your youth;
> A lovable doe! A sweet little mountain goat!
> May her breasts always intoxicate you!
> May you ever find rapture in loving her!
> (Prov. 5:18–19, Anchor Bible)

The ancient Jews approved of physical passion between spouses since they believed that natural forces are a good creation of God. They thought divine grandeur could be sensed through pleasant as well as painful experiences. Post-Biblical Jewish sayings express well this point of view. An ancient rabbi commented: "A man will some day have to give an account to God for all the good things which his eyes beheld and of which he refused to enjoy."[7] Robert Browning, after noting the psychosomatic holism of a distinguished medieval rabbi, wrote: "Let us cry, 'All good things / Are ours, nor soul helps flesh more, now, than flesh helps soul!' "[8] Traditional values are also articulated in the prayer that concludes the Jewish wedding ceremony: "Blessed be thou, O Lord, . . . who hast created joy and gladness, groom and bride, jubilation and exultation, pleasure and delight, love, brotherliness, peace, and friendliness. . . . Blessed be thou, O Lord, who makest rejoice the groom with his bride."

If sensuousness in male-female relationships was encouraged in the Song of Songs and in the Jewish community that interpreted it, why is it that for most of Judeo-Christian history this dominant motif of the Song has been muted, if not silenced altogether? To answer this question adequately, we must examine post-Biblical Jewish and Christian treatments of the Song.

DUAL INTERPRETATIONS IN JUDAISM

No reference is made to the Song of Songs in the earliest writings by Jews after the Old Testament era. There are no overt allusions to it in the writings of Philo, Josephus, or the New Testament. The first mention of the Song is in rabbinic literature and there it carries a double meaning. In the Mishnah it is associated with the traditional wedding dance in which maidens participated. The "daughters of Jerusalem went forth to dance in the vineyard" and sang: "Young man, lift up your eyes and see whom you would choose for yourself." In addition to this literal interpretation, that rabbinic passage also gives the Song symbolic meaning. Solomon's wedding is interpreted to mean the giving of the Torah, and "the day of the gladness of his heart" (ch. 3:11) is taken to mean the building of the Temple.[9]

Around A.D. 100 Akiba said: "He who sings the Song of Songs in wine taverns, treating it as if it were a vulgar song, forfeits his share in the world to come."[10] What did he mean by that warning? Akiba held that "You shall love your neighbor as yourself" was the most fundamental truth in the Mosaic legislation.[11] Assuming that he viewed one's spouse as at least as worthy as one's less intimate neighbor, the rabbi was concerned that the marital love expressed in the Song be given the dignity it deserved. Akiba boldly stated that, far from being a bawdy song, with only a secular significance, the Song of Songs was the "holy of holies" of the sacred writings. He claimed that the Song had long been treasured by most members of the Jewish community.[12]

There is no evidence that the ancient Jews rejected the literal sense of a writing either before or after accepting it as authoritative Scripture. The unadorned meaning remained prominent after canonization, even though speculations about additional theological and moral

meanings were given. It was contrary to the respect which Jews gave
to the plain meaning of their literature to accept only the allegorical
meaning. Even Philo of Alexandria, who was the most allegorically
prone of all Jews, did not discard its literal meaning.[13] R. P. C.
Hanson has rightly observed: "Rabbinic allegory is characterized by
the fact that it never for a moment impugns the validity of the literal
sense."[14]

The earliest known Jewish commentary on the entire Song of
Songs is in a targum dating from the sixth century A.D. Without
denying the literal meaning, that commentary erects an allegorical
superstructure over it.[15] Following an analogy frequently found in
the prophets, the groom symbolizes Yahweh and his bride is Judaism.
A similar dual interpretation is later found in a commentary on the
Song by Abraham ben Isaac in the fourteenth century.[16] Israel
Abrahams has stated that the Song was probably the most popular
Scriptural book for medieval Jews.[17]

GRECO-CHRISTIAN ALLEGORIZATION

Among Gentiles, allegorization had a distinctly different purpose
than it had in the Jewish community. Frequently those Greek intel-
lectuals who found odious the obvious meaning of some poetry re-
vered in their culture substituted a basically opposing meaning to the
objectionable lines. Allegorical interpretation can be traced to such
early Greek philosophers as Xenophanes, Pythagoras, and Plato, who
were offended by the alleged sexual activity and other an-
thropomorphic behavior of the Homeric gods.[18]

The Stoics were the chief exponents of allegorism in the Hellenistic era. Believing that a man must be dispassionate to be truly moral,
they were much embarrassed by the divine models of morality in
Greek culture. By allegorizing the myths, the Stoics transposed the
appearance of carnal passion into an acceptable discarnate spirituality.[19]

In Christianity, the Song of Songs received attention after the
center of influence of the church moved from Jerusalem westward
into the Greco-Roman social order. Following the destruction of the
Jewish state, ethical standards affecting the church came more from

Gentile than from Jewish culture. It was commonplace in pagan religion and philosophy to associate purity with sexual renunciation. Those Christians with a Roman background had come to respect the abstaining vestal virgins as exemplars of holy behavior. Also, in the Hellenistic cults of the Eastern Mediterranean, celibacy was associated with the sacred.

This general contrast between Jews and Gentiles in their outlook regarding sexuality precipitated a dilemma among Gentile Christians with respect to the Song of Songs. In the second century some of them rejected the book as authoritative sacred writing. Marcion, for example, partly because of his zeal for sexual asceticism, advocated that Christians discard not only the Song but also the entire collection of Hebrew Scripture. None of those books belonged in the Christian canon, he believed, because they wrongly affirmed that the good God had created nature and natural impulses. Marcion's anti-Jewish position was too extreme for most Christians. Although they were uneasy regarding the Song, they realized that it would be better to accept the entire Hebrew canon than to weigh each book individually to determine whether it was holy or profane. That decision stifled dissent, but it left Christian interpreters with the acute embarrassment of having to explain a book that seemed to praise passionate sexual activity in a period when that was generally believed to be the root of much evil.

Allegory was brought to the rescue. Having noticed the effective way in which the philosophers had recast the sensuous gods of Homer and Hesiod into ethereal ideals, Christian theologians were quick to follow their example. Thus the sensuous celebration by a couple in the Song of Songs was interpreted as prayer communion between a pious Christian and his ever-loving God. Thus the passionate paeans which the church had inherited from the authoritative books of the synagogue were converted into what was thought to be a harmless mysticism. Indeed, the Song came to be reckoned as one of the most important books by sexually ascetic Christians because allegorical sermons on it showed how the dishonorable libidinous drives could be pommeled and sublimated. Jean Leclercq, an authority on monasticism, has called the Song "the book which was most read and most frequently commented on in the medieval cloister."[20] From the third

century until the nineteenth, Christian interpreters have usually
treated the Song as an allegory, with each finding hidden beneath the
sexual imagery his preconceived Christological and ascetic doctrines.

Hippolytus, a Roman who flourished around A.D. 200, is the first
Christian on record to have allegorized the Song of Songs. The
fragments of his commentary that remain show how he transformed
the Song into a vehicle for conveying an austere ethic. Those who
crucify their fleshly desires are elevated to the "hill of frankincense"
(ch. 4:6). "The king has brought me into his chambers" (ch. 1:4) is
interpreted to mean that Jesus has brought Christians to whom he
is wedded into the church. Switching his symbolism, Hippolytus has
Christians sucking from the bride's two breasts (ch. 4:5), which
represent the Old and New Covenants.[21]

Origen, a younger contemporary of Hippolytus, may have been
influenced by the earlier allegorist. Both shared the conviction that
the caressing king connotes Jesus, and his bride represents either the
corporate church or the individual Christian. Origen composed sermons and a ten-volume commentary on the Song of Songs which is
only in small part extant. In the prologue to the commentary he
warned passionate persons not to read further. He regarded the Song
as safe reading only for older persons who are no longer troubled by
sexual desires. "Everyone who is not yet rid of the vexations of flesh
and blood and has not ceased to feel the passion of his bodily nature
should refrain completely from reading this book."

Those words display Origen's proneness toward extremism. When
he was young he took too literally Jesus' hyperbole about cutting off
bodily members that cause one to sin, and thus castrated himself.
Later in life he took too figuratively the Song of Songs and rejected
its literal meaning. Eunuch Origen was sure that God never intended
the book to be understood except as a purely spiritual drama of the
inner life. The dark bride (ch. 1:5) represents the Christian whose
stain of carnal sin has not been washed away.[22] Her desire for the
groom's left hand under her head while being fondled by his right
hand (ch. 2:6) means that the church longs for the glory and eternity
of Jesus.[23] These are samples of the way in which Origen ingeniously
denatured the sexual sentiments of the Song. In the course of his
writing he made this plea: "We earnestly beg the hearers of these

things to mortify their carnal senses. They must not take anything of what has been said with reference to bodily functions but rather employ them for grasping those divine senses of the inner man."[24]

Origen introduced Plato's interpretation of love into Christianity by means of his Song of Songs allegory. Plato had distinguished between sensual and nonphysical loves.[25] Origen wrote in a Platonic manner: "There is a love of the flesh which comes from Satan, and there is also another love, belonging to the Spirit, which has its origin in God; and nobody can be possessed by the two loves. . . . If you have despised all bodily things . . . then you can acquire spiritual love."[26]

The sacred marriage mystery of Hellenistic religions[27] was an even more immediate influence upon Origen than Plato's theory of love. Adolf Harnack has pointed out that Origen was indebted to those pagan Gnostics who treated the divine Spirit as the exclusive bridegroom of the devotee.[28]

The Acts of Thomas, which reflects Gnostic currents of Origen's day,[29] affords an excellent illustration of the heavenly union that is claimed by those who shun fleshly entanglements. In one episode an earthly wedding becomes the setting for the reunuciation of sexual intercourse. According to that apocryphal book, a divine epiphany followed a wedding prayer given by the apostle Thomas. Jesus appeared and proclaimed: "If you abandon this filthy intercourse you become holy temples, pure and free from afflictions and pains both manifest and hidden, and you will not be girt about with cares for life and for children, the end of which is destruction." Consequently, that night the terrified couple "refrained from the filthy passion" and afterward the bride claimed: "I have set at naught this man and this marriage which passes away from before my eyes, because I am bound in another marriage. I have had no intercourse with a short-lived husband . . . because I am yoked with the true man."[30] In another story the identity of the immortal bridegroom is made explicit. Thomas advised another wife to abstain from "horrid intercourse," for it leads to "eternal damnation." Accepting his advice, she repelled the sexual advances of a kind husband with these contemptuous words: "He whom I love is better than you and your possessions. . . . Jesus himself will set me free from the shameful deeds which I did with you. . . . You are a bridegroom who passes away and is destroyed, but Jesus is a true bridegroom, abiding immortal for ever."[31]

In the fourth century, when monasticism was undergoing rapid development, the ideas of nonsensual sacred marriage which Origen imported from pagan Hellenism became enormously popular. In a preface written by Jerome for a translation of Origen's sermons on the Song of Songs, that Latin scholar wrote: "While Origen surpassed all writers in his other books, in his Song of Songs he surpassed himself."[32] The Song was viewed by Jerome as a poem praising virgins who mortify the flesh. He informed them that Jesus would titillate those who detest physical relationships with other men: "Ever let the Bridegroom fondle you. . . . He will put his hand through the opening and will touch your body. And you will arise trembling and cry, 'I am lovesick.' "[33] While Jerome polemicized against coitus on the physical level, he was engrossed in it on a fantasy level.

Aware that a novice might miss what he saw in the Song of Songs, Jerome prescribed that a girl should not study the book until other studies were completed. "If she were to read it at the beginning," he asserted, "she might be harmed by not perceiving that it was the song of a spiritual wedding expressed in fleshly language."[34] In accordance with his motto, *omnis coitus impurus*,[35] Jerome assured those who withstood sexual defilement until death that they would be rewarded by Jesus their bridegroom. He will say to each one to whom he is married who is resting in a grave: "Rise up, my fair one, my dove, and come; for lo, the winter is past, the rain is over and gone."[36] By inverted interpretations such as this, monk Jerome took the book of Scripture that posed the greatest threat to sexual asceticism and converted it into an asset.

Gregory of Nyssa, a prominent Greek bishop, allegorized the Song of Songs in his fifteen sermons on that book. He praised Origen's treatment of the Song and held that those who interpret it literally are obscene and will be punished in hell. The entire book, according to Gregory, deals exclusively with an exchange between the soul and God. But only when the soul becomes passionless can it become fully united with God. Gregory shows his Platonism in such affirmations as these: "The love of God can only arise from what is contrary to carnal desire"; and "The life of flesh and blood must be mortified by the contemplation of spiritual reality."[37] The bride's testimony, "I slept, but my heart was awake" (ch. 5:2), is interpreted to mean: "The soul, enjoying alone the contemplation of Being, will not awake for anything that arouses sensual pleasure. After lulling to sleep every bodily motion, it receives the vision of God in a divine wakefulness with pure and naked intuition."[38]

Ambrose, a contemporary of Jerome and Gregory, also found in the Song of Songs a vivid account of the Christian who turns away from the pleasures of the flesh in order to sport with Jesus. Accordingly, "O that you would kiss me!" (ch. 1:2) refers to the Lord's faithful who had long waited with ardent hope for his coming.[39] After his incarnation, this invitation was extended: "Come with me from Lebanon" (ch. 4:8). To accept Jesus' call, Ambrose contended, involves renouncing the world and concentrating all affections on him.[40] It is the virgins who are properly prepared for their heavenly spouse. "My breasts were like towers" (ch. 8:10) refers to those whose sexual organs are impregnable and thereby "with unspotted chastity keep the couch of the Lord holy."[41] The words "Eat, O friends, and drink" (ch. 5:1) mean that the devout are invited to the Eucharist, where they can "eat, drink, and be inebriated."[42] Ambrose also found in the Song various references to the mother of Jesus. For example, "I am a rose of Sharon" (ch. 2:1) is taken to be Jesus' claim that he budded forth from a virgin's womb.[43]

Bernard of Clairvaux, the towering church leader of the twelfth century, is principally known as a writer by his allegorical interpretation of the Song of Songs. He prepared eighty-six sermons on that book, averaging more than two sermons per verse for the first two chapters completed! Like the medieval alchemist, he was obsessed with a desire to transform material which he regarded as base into something precious. He had contempt for the flesh and females and was determined to show that the life of the spirit was unalloyed with sex. Following previous Christian allegorists, he thought that only a vile person would interpret the Song as an expression of natural feelings. He urged: "Take heed that you bring chaste ears to this discourse of love; and when you think of these two lovers, remember always that not a man and a woman are to be thought of, but the Word of God and a Soul."[44] Thus he viewed the love song as a mystic cryptogram that is unlocked when read as Orphic literature. The bride's boast, "I am black but beautiful" (ch. 1:5), is interpreted to portray the contrast between the ugliness of the soul in the present corporeal entombment and the luster it will have when it wings away into eternity.[45] "I sought him, but found him not" (ch. 3:1) means, according to Bernard, that our not finding God is due to our being "imprisoned in the flesh, sunk in mire."[46]

As with other allegorists, Bernard's alleged exposition tells us nothing about the Scriptural text but rather exposes the turmoil of the mystic composer. One of his contemporaries relates a telling episode from the life of Bernard that shows his dread of sex. During his youth an exchange of admiring glances with a girl triggered an erection. Because he associated sensual passion with the fire of hell, he plunged into a pond of icy water to extinguish his burning concupiscence. When his tumescence subsided, he resolved that he would become a celibate.[47]

"If you drive nature out with a pitchfork," Horace sagaciously observed, "she will find a way back."[48] Bernard's repressed erotic urges resulted in a destructive flood of dark passion in later life. By means of an inverted sublimation he channeled his ardent desire for the opposite sex into a hatred of alleged heretics and infidels. In particular he had an antipathy toward Peter Abelard that was in large part due to a different assessment of human love. Abelard did not believe that natural urges were sinful or that sexuality was contaminated from Adam's fall. He inquired: "If cohabitation with a wife and the enjoyment of pleasant things were allowed us in Paradise from the first day of our creation without guilt being incurred, who may argue that these things are now sinful, provided only that we do not exceed the limits of our permission?"[49]

Bernard was outraged by Abelard's criticism of the Augustinian doctrine of original sin.[50] Consequently, he requested Pope Innocent II to exterminate the "fox destroying the Lord's vineyard."[51] He no doubt learned from Augustine how to appropriate imagery from the Song of Songs to attack anyone who deviated from the prevailing outlook of the church. The Bishop of Hippo had interpreted "Your teeth are like a flock of shorn ewes" (ch. 4:2) as an allusion to the teeth of saints tearing at heretics! He confessed that it gave him pleasure to envisage Christians as "cutting off men from their errors and transferring them to the church after their hardness has been softened as if by being bitten and chewed."[52]

As a result of Bernard's efforts, Abelard was excommunicated and his books were burned.[53] It is unlikely that Bernard was satisfied with this punishment, for he proclaimed in a sermon on the Song of Songs that "heretics should be put to death."[54] Peter the Venerable, who lamented Bernard's self-appointed role as heresy hunter, wrote him these candid words: "You perform all the difficult religious duties; you fast, you watch, you suffer; but you will not endure the easy ones —you do not love."[55] Arthur C. McGiffert points even more acutely to the irony of Bernard's character: "For all his praise of love he was a violent hater."[56]

Bernard used his sermons on the Song of Songs to chastize his enemies outside the church as well as within. He thought it was a Christian's duty to despise those assumed to be rejected by God. With regard to a person commonly recognized as an enemy, he asserted: "It is necessary that you think of him not as almost nothing but as nothing at all."[57] Consequently, Bernard wrote numerous letters to influential Europeans urging that the Moslems in Palestine be altogether crushed. In one he exclaimed:

> What multitudes of sinners, confessing their offences with sorrow, have in that Holy Land been reconciled to God, since the swords of Christian warriors drove thence the foul pagans! . . . The Living God has charged me to proclaim that he will take vengeance upon such as refuse to defend him against his foes. To arms, then! Let a holy indignation animate you to the combat, and let the cry of Jeremiah reverberate through Christendom: "Cursed be he that withholdeth his sword from blood."[58]

Captivated by Bernard's ascetic appearance and fiery rhetoric, thousands joined to form the Second Crusade. At Chartres he was chosen as its commander-in-chief, but because of his age he declined the honor.[59]

It has been recognized that devotion to aggressive war becomes for some persons a substitute for frustrated love.[60] Bernard provides an excellent case study of one who substituted the arrows of Mars for the darts of Cupid. "Make war, not love" might have been an appropriate motto for that saint!

Strangely enough, Bernard has been singled out by some as one of the most Christlike persons in church history. In his own era, Dante regarded him as the supreme guide to the heavenly realm.[61] A Protestant theologian of the present century concluded his lengthy study of Bernard with this typical evaluation: "One does not know where else to look for a more lofty and shining exhibition of the power of faith."[62] If Bernard exemplified what in recent years has been called the golden age of Western spirituality,[63] it is indeed a sad commentary on the course of Christianity.

In late medieval Catholicism, allegorical interpretations of the Song of Songs were popular among both the unscholarly mystics and the philosophical theologians. The writings of celibate Jan van Ruysbroek are an example of the former. The Song was a main source of his imagery for expressing the delectable climax of the soul's intercourse with the divine Bridegroom. Thomas Aquinas exemplifies scholasticism's appreciation of the Song in that it provided the text for his last sermon before his death. A medieval hagiographer tells of that event in this way: "It was indeed appropriate that the great worker in the school of the Church should terminate his teaching on that song of eternal glory; that such a master in that school, when about to pass from the prison of the body to the heavenly wedding feast, should discourse on that bridal union of the Church with Christ her Spouse."[64]

The Song of Songs has continued to be principally interpreted as an allegory in the modern history of Roman Catholicism. In the Douay Version, which served for several centuries as the approved English translation for Catholics, there is an unusual treatment of one verse of the Song. Following the Vulgate's mistranslation, the bridegroom's words read:

> Under the apple tree I raised thee up:
> There thy mother was corrupted,
> There she was deflowered that bore thee.
>   (Ch. 8:5, Douay Version)

Jerome, who considered even marital sexuality defiling, read his own ascetic bias into his Latin translation. To compound that inaccuracy, the Douay Bible added this Christological annotation: *"Under the apple tree I raised thee up;* that is that Christ redeemed the Gentiles at the foot of the cross, where the synagogue of the Jews (the mother church) *was corrupted* by their denying him, and crucifying him." However, the Hebrew and Septuagint texts should be translated thus:

> Under the fruit trees I roused you:
> There your mother brought you forth,
> There she who bore you was in labor.

During the past decade some Catholic exegetes have recognized that the Song of Songs was originally intended to be understood as lyrics of human lovers and should now be interpreted as such.[65] However, the comments in *The Jerusalem Bible* and *A New Catholic Commentary* suggest that most Roman Catholic interpreters today retain an allegorical interpretation.[66] In the former, for example, Jesus is found hidden in the image of the bride's "brother" (ch. 8:1) and Mary's Immaculate Conception is discovered in the description of the bride as "unblemished" (ch. 4:7). That Marian doctrine implies that ordinary mortal conception is soiled with sin, so a bias against sex has not yet been purged from the Catholic interpretation of the Song.

Protestant scholars also generally upheld an allegorical interpretation of the Song of Songs until the past century. Luther was inconsistent in this regard. On the one hand he expressed himself in this manner: "So far as allegories are concerned Origen is a prince, a king; he filled the whole Bible with secret interpretations of this kind, which aren't worth a damn. The reason was that they all followed their own conceits, thoughts and opinions, as they thought fit."[67] However, Luther criticized any who might be tempted to interpret the Song literally and could not resist imposing on it his political bent. Offering a unique interpretation, he claimed that the book was written to encourage peasants to be obedient to their divinely ordained rulers.[68] Hence, "Stir not up nor awaken love" (ch. 8:4) means: "You cities, whoever you are under this worship and government of God, take care to be quiet and peaceful, lest you incite disturbance."[69]

English-speaking Protestants have been influenced for several centuries by the headings provided by the translators of the King James Version of the Bible. For example, "The church having a taste of Christ's love" is the interpretive clue given for these sentiments by the bride: "My beloved put in his hand by the hole of the door, and my bowels were moved for him" (ch. 5:4). Christ affectionately reciprocates with imagery such as this: "The joints of thy thighs are like jewels. . . . Thy navel is like a round goblet, which wanteth not liquor" (ch. 7:1–3). The church's prayer for Christ's Second Coming is found in this verse: "Make haste, my beloved; and be thou like to a roe or to a young hart upon the mountains of spices" (ch. 8:14).

Presbyterians and Methodists have been warned by high authority to avoid the plain meaning of the Song of Songs. In the seventeenth century, the Westminster Assembly censured interpreters who have blasphemously "received it as a hot carnall pamphlet formed by some loose Apollo or Cupid."[70] John Wesley informed his followers:

> The description of this bridegroom and bride is such as could not with decency be used or meant concerning Solomon and Pharaoh's daughter; that many expressions and descriptions, if applied to them, would be absurd and monstrous; and that it therefore follows that this book is to be understood allegorically concerning that spiritual love and marriage which is between Christ and his church.[71]

A Song of Human Love

Throughout most of the history of the church it has been regarded as false and morally pernicious to interpret the Song of Songs literally. However, around A.D. 400, there was one clergyman in the Latin church and one in the Greek church who advocated that the plain meaning of the Song be respected. In Rome, during the heyday of sexual asceticism, Jovinian urged that the marital state not be denigrated by commending those who make vows of perpetual virginity as having the morally superior life-style. He appealed to Scripture to show that the married were not, in the sight of God, inferior to the virgins. In particular he claimed that the Song is full of the idea that marital sexuality is hallowed.[72]

Latin prelates were incensed by Jovinian's position. They saw it as subversive to the monastic movement they so ardently supported. Consequently Jerome, in a long diatribe, attacked both Jovinian and the sanctity of marriage. He used allegorical counterfeit in an attempt to reject Jovinian's appeal to the Song of Songs as evidence that sexual expression can be as holy as repression. Jerome held that the true meaning of the Song is diametrically opposite to the literal meaning: the book is designed to teach that sexual abstinence is the way to avoid sin. Bishop Ambrose and Pope Siricius joined Jerome in condemning Jovinian for "heresy" and "blasphemy" at council meetings in Milan and Rome. Ambrose, who had allegorized the Song to embroider his sexual asceticism, found Jovinian's Biblical interpretation hideous. Siricius, who referred to marital sexuality of those in holy orders as "obscene cupidity,"[73] likewise rejected Jovinian's assessment.

In the Eastern church, Theodore of Mopsuestia protested the allegorization of Scripture because it perverted its plain meaning.[74] In particular, he asserted that the Song of Songs was a love song in which Solomon celebrated his marriage with an Egyptian bride.[75] Doubtless his mode of interpretation was influenced by his belief that sexual desire was not inherently impure. His openness to the positive values of sexuality is evidenced in his belief that even the sinless Jesus had fleshly impulses.[76] Theodore's position was too radical for his ascetic milieu. Even his student, Bishop Theodoret, declared that Theodore's interpretation of the Song was "not even fitting in the mouth of a crazy woman."[77] A century later, in 553, the Second Council of Constantinople condemned Theodore's interpretation and anathematized the bishop.[78] Understandably, for the next millennium no other churchmen were brazen enough to interpret the Song as passionate love poetry about a man and a maiden.

It was not until John Calvin rejected the allegorical mode of interpretation that scholars began to reappraise the Song of Songs. That sixteenth-century Reformer forthrightly stated his position in this way:

Origen, and many others along with him, have seized the occasion of torturing Scripture, in every possible manner, away from the true sense. They concluded that the literal sense is too mean and poor, and that, under the outer bark of the letter, there lurk deeper mysteries, which cannot be extracted but by beating out allegories. . . . [But] the true meaning of Scripture is the natural and obvious meaning.[79]

Sebastian Castellio, who studied under Calvin, was convinced that the Song of Songs should be understood literally, but he was not convinced that it was worthy to stand in the canon of Holy Scripture. He is reported to have called it "a lascivious and obscene poem in which Solomon described his indecent amours."[80] Calvin strongly disagreed with Castellio's moral judgment on this matter, and this can be attributed to their different attitudes toward sexuality. Calvin stated, in his exposition of I Cor., ch. 7: "Conjugal intercourse is a thing that is pure, honorable, and holy." Accordingly, he held that the Song was an unsullied nuptial ode similar to Ps. 45. In both, Calvin argued, Solomon sings of the beauty of the Creator's handicraft, and so it is presumptuous for anyone to reject what has been declared good by God. Calvin also saw in those historical wedding lyrics a premonition of the quality of love that later would form a covenantal bond between Christ and his church.[81] He did not think it improper to associate the marriage-bed celebration with the deepest divine manifestation of love. So, rather than banishing the Song from the inspired canon, Calvin used his influence to deny ordination to Castellio and expel him from his teaching position in Geneva.

Castellio's outlook made sense to those who placed negative valuation on both allegorical and sexual expression. An example of this attitude is found in eighteenth-century scholar William Whiston, who held that the Song of Songs is filled with earthy erotic exchanges and that therefore it is altogether out of place in a collection of sacred literature.[82]

Edmund Spenser, an English Puritan, seems to have been the first scholar to accept Calvin's position that the Song of Songs is both divinely inspired and a song of human love. He translated the book[83] and alluded to it frequently in his poems.[84] The Song is especially prominent in the lovely poem he composed in 1594 to commemorate his own wedding. When making an inventory of female features, he used the Song as the source for some of his images. Thus Spenser describes his "truest, turtle dove" in this way:

> Her goodly eyes lyke Saphyres shining bright,
> Her forehead yvory white,
> Her cheekes lyke apples which the sun hath rudded,
> Her lips lyke cherryes charming men to byte,
> Her brest like to a bowle of creame uncrudded,
> Her paps like lyllies budded,
> Her snowie necke lyke to a marble towre,
> And all her body like a pallace fayre,
> Ascending uppe with many a stately stayre,
> To honors seat and chastities sweet bowre.[85]

Having disciplined his desires for some forty years as a bachelor, Spenser looked forward to his wedding as a consecrated consummation:

> Never had man more joyfull day then this, . . .
> This day for ever to me holy is.[86]

It was not until two centuries after Spenser that a commentary was produced in which the Song of Songs was interpreted as a charming expression of natural love that points to the holiness of human relations. This was accomplished by Johann Gottfried von Herder, a leader in eighteenth-century German Romanticism, who was attracted to poetry in which the divine is enmeshed with nature and human feelings. He found in the Song a sequence of independent ditties extolling sentimental and physical love as pure.[87] Owing in large part to Herder's influence, Johann Wolfgang von Goethe came to have an appreciation for the beauty of unembellished nature. Goethe showed the influence of his mentor when he claimed that the Song is "the most tender and inimitable expression of graceful yet passionate love that has come down to us. . . . The principal theme is an ardent longing of youthful hearts, seeking, finding, repulsing, attracting, under various most simple conditions."[88]

In the centuries since Herder a number of novel interpretations of the Song of Songs have been advanced, but few have been convinced by them. The most scholarly review of these modern interpretations has been given by H. H. Rowley. He concludes with a judgment that is essentially the same as that of Theodore, Jovinian, Spenser, and Herder: "The view I adopt finds in it nothing but what it appears to be, lovers' songs, expressing their delight in one another and the warm emotion of their hearts. All of the other views find in the Song what they bring to it." Rowley thinks that the Song deserves to be included in the authoritative literature of the Christian religion even though it is a duet of an erotic couple. He comments: "The Church has always consecrated the union of man and woman in matrimony, and taught that marriage is a divine ordinance, and it is not unfitting that a book which expresses the spiritual and physical emotions on which matrimony rests should be given a place in the canon of Scripture."[89]

CONCLUSION

"There is no instinct that has been so maligned, suppressed, abused, and distorted by religious teaching as the instinct of sex."[90] This observation of Dora (Mrs. Bertrand) Russell has been amply confirmed by the hermeneutical history of the Song of Songs. However, she is indiscriminate in criticizing religious teaching generally for mistreatment of sexuality. Judaism has from the beginning been distinctively different from those religions which give the impression that coitus is at best a lamentable necessity for human survival. Jewish novelist Herman Wouk has rightly discerned that the Western notion that sexual intercourse is somehow wrong "is the ghost of crushed paganism rising out of the marble of overthrown temples to Venus in the walls and floors of early Christian churches."[91]

With respect to the Song of Songs, Theodore of Mopsuestia was the only church leader of stature during Christianity's first fifteen hundred years who appreciated the original meaning of the Song and had the courage to go against the strong currents of sexual asceticism in his culture in defending his position. Although he was condemned as a heretic, respect for his hermeneutics is now increasing. McGiffert has justifiably called him "the greatest exegete of the ancient church."[92]

Interpreting the Song of Songs as lyrics of human love has confronted prelates with an embarrassing dilemma. If, on the one hand, the book's prima facie meaning was acknowledged, then the established assumption about the superiority of those persons in the church devoted to lifelong sexual abstinence is called in question. On the other hand, if the book was renounced, what would prohibit Christians from calling into question other Biblical books which had been appealed to as authoritative? Given these practical problems, it is easy to understand why allegory was brought to the rescue even though there is no clue within the Song to suggest that is was originally composed with another meaning in mind. Polonius' wry words are germane: "Though this be madness, yet there is method in it."

Allegorists were able to do much more than uphold the dogma of inspiration of all alleged "Holy Scriptures" and the doctrine that fleshly indulgence is morally inferior to marital renunciation. They were able to cull phrases from the Song of Songs that could communicate an ego-satisfying private mysticism that had been imported from Greek religion. Orphism, which was transmitted by Pythagoreanism, Platonism, and Stoicism into Gentile Christianity, emphasized that those who rigorously subdued their emotions would be rewarded by suprarational ecstasy and by union of their souls with the ultimate Spirit. Even though the notion of solitary salvation was foreign to the dominant thrust of Biblical religion, allegorists realized that symbols from the Song could be appropriated for the ethereal "flight of the alone to the Alone."

Perverse interpretations of the Song of Songs culminated with Bernard of Clairvaux. That monk, who has been designated the "Mellifluous Doctor," concealed some anti-Christian poison in his honeyed teachings. Bernard said: "When God loves, he desires nothing else than to be loved."[93] In his famous ladder of love he omits love of another human. The rungs ascend thus: love of self for self's sake; love of God for self's sake; love of God for God's sake; love of self for God's sake.[94] Bernard overlooked these strong words of the New Testament: "If God so loved us, we in turn ought to love one another. . . . If a man says, 'I love God,' while hating his brother, he is a liar. If he does not love the brother whom he has seen, it cannot be that he loves God whom he has not seen" (I John 4:11, 20).

Claude Tresmontant, rightly regarding love as fundamental to the outlook of Biblical religion, states: "To think that one loves God if one's love does not first go to individual existent beings, is a delusion."[95] Bernard's love was defective because he could not appreciate the love of spouses and because of his hatred for all who deviated from his narrow doctrine of how God must be worshiped. His disdain for women, his contempt toward Abelard, and his conviction that the only good Moslem is a dead Moslem show that being "high" on Jesus drugged him to the extent that he was not fully aware of his own loveless attitudes.

Whereas Bernard regarded fleshly affection as vile, the callous lack of affection toward wife and fellowman is regarded as a vice in the New Testament.[96] The early Christians believed that the way to God was through participation in, not abstention from, intimate love. Had Bernard been more open to the quintessence of New Testament ethics—that we love others as Jesus loved his companions—he could have found other books of the Old Testament more objectionable than the one in which the love theme percolates throughout. In the Greek Bible, it is the brief book of Song of Songs that most frequently uses the term *agapē*, which became a key term for the New Testament writers.

There are several books of Jewish Scriptures which, from the standpoint of the *agapē* ethic, are obscene in their plain meaning. It is a pity that Bernard and his fellow allegorists did not select them for mutilation. Some candidates are Joshua, which boasts extravagantly of merciless slaughter in the name of Yahweh during a war of conquest, and the books of Obadiah, Nahum, and Esther, which gloat over the bloody destruction of ethnic foes.

The defect of most Christian allegorical interpretations, in contrast to Jewish allegories of the Song of Songs, is not that they find heavenly overtones in the language of lovers, but that they find little or no religious significance in natural beauty, emotional feeling, and physical relations. Although God is not mentioned in the Song, there is in the book an implicit praise to the one who has created the exquisite handiwork of the out-of-doors and has encouraged his creatures to enjoy spontaneous wooing. For the prominent Christian allegorists, it was unthinkable that honeymoon caressing could be hallowed. For them, as moral dualists, there could be no traffic between sensuous contact and spiritual union. Love of God was antithetical to sexual love. Such a doctrine finds no legitimate ground in any of the Judeo-Christian Scriptures.

Only those who come to the Song with the preconceived idea that the portrayal of lovemaking is smutty find the book repugnant. To render a New Testament proverb negatively: To the impure, all things are impure. The lesson that the apostle Peter learned is apropos here. After puzzling through a vision he received, he realized that he had been wrong in reckoning as unclean what God had made clean (Acts 10:15). He came to realize that all men, as well as all meats, are pure creations. A further implication of Peter's experience is that the sensate as well as the intangible aspects of the human self are hallowed.

The traditional allegories drawn from the Song of Songs must be rejected because they violate the basic canon of literary interpretation, namely, they attempt to read out of a work what is contrary to the writer's point of view. Moreover, they advocate a false psychology and an unbiblical theology. They attempt to split off the *psyche* from the *sōma*, placing high value on some nonmaterial soul substance, while showing contempt for bodily functions. With respect to theology, the allegories presuppose that natural functioning is an unfit sphere for divine manifestation.

In place of a sickly, discarnate mysticism, the holiness of the erotic should be recovered. Passion and rapture should not be excluded from the spiritual any more than fidelity and discipline should be excluded from the sexual. It is incongruous to think that earthly ties should be drained of their carnality in order to be acceptable to the "Word made flesh."

When Lutheran pastor Dietrich Bonhoeffer was engaged to be married, he related this experience to the Song of Songs. Before his martyrdom in a Nazi concentration camp he grandly affirmed:

> God requires that we should love him eternally with our whole hearts, yet not so as to compromise or diminish our earthly affections, but as a kind of *cantus firmus* to which the other melodies of life provide the counterpoint. Earthly affection is one of these

contrapuntal themes, a theme which enjoys an autonomy of its own. Even the Bible can find room for the Song of Songs, and one could hardly have a more passionate and sensual love than is there portrayed (see 7.6). It is a good thing that that book is included in the Bible as a protest against those who believe that Christianity stands for the restraint of passion.

These sentiments display Bonhoeffer's conviction that Christians have erred in that "we read the New Testament far too little on the basis of the Old." He was aware that the God of Israel was the "beyond" in the midst of our human loves.[97]

The most sensuous book in Scripture and in all the writings of antiquity is the Song of Songs. As a book of religion it is at least as sublime as a number of other Biblical books. It tells of the joyfulness and constancy of genuine affection. It glorifies a bond that is sweeter than honey and stronger than a lion. The affirmation, "Love is strong as death" (ch. 8:6) is excelled only by the New Testament proclamation that love is even stronger than death. The apostles believed love to be the most indestructible quality in the universe, for God is love. In Part II we will explore the way in which that love was incarnated in the life of Jesus and in the sacramental religion which he founded.

3

Aspects of Jesus' Personality

THE COMPLETE humanity of Jesus has been only theoretically accepted in the Christian tradition. Creeds of the church affirm that he was truly man, but for most Christians this means little more than that he was born and felt pain; he ate, slept, and died. The fully human emotional and psychological life of Jesus has never been adequately explored. Little attention has been given to Jesus as Walt Whitman saw him: "turbulent, fleshly, sensual . . . no stander above men or women or apart from them."[1]

Since the founder of Christianity is also its supreme exemplar, it is important to attempt to comprehend Jesus' sensitivity to several matters that closely affect all people: the emotions of laughter and anger, work and leisure, and sexual realities. It will be seen that the conception Christians have of Jesus' life-style has often been the reverse of the New Testament portrait. However, his authentic life-style was in line with what is now recommended for optimum personal functioning by even those psychologists devoid of Christian bias.

LAUGHTER AND ANGER

It is now recognized that a sense of humor is essential for healthy human personality. Sigmund Freud devoted considerable attention to the analysis of humor, treating it as man's best safety valve.[2] Man has frequently been partially defined as an animal that laughs. Humans are the only jokers in nature: even the so-called "laughing" hyena is not at all tickled. The uniquely human quality of humor is a by-product of man's ability to distinguish his ideal self from his actual self. Humor comes from his awareness of the gap between his high pretensions and his pathetic behavior. Humor is a moral necessity, for it helps to deflate the haughty and give a modest self-appraisal.

Yet in spite of these commendable qualities, humor has often been scorned in the Christian tradition. Basil and Chrysostom, two outstanding fourth-century Greek churchmen, wrote about the wickedness of laughter. "This world is not a theater in which we can laugh ... but a place to groan and by this inherit the kingdom," commented Chrysostom; "when you see persons laughing, reflect that those teeth that grin now will one day have to sustain that most dreadful wailing and gnashing."[3] Centuries later another saint, Ignatius Loyola, also rejected humor. He decreed that members of the Jesuit order, which he founded, should accept this discipline: "I shall not laugh or say anything that will cause laughter."[4]

Protestants have also had their share of humorless leaders. "The life of a Christian man is a perpetuall studie and exercise of mortifying the fleshe untille it be utterly slaine," wrote one of them in 1577. John Northbrooke admonished that there should be "insteade of playing, praying; insteade of dauncing, repenting; for joye, sorrowe; for laughing, mourning; for myrth, sadnesse."[5] Francis Asbury, the apostle of early Methodism in America, denounced those who dared to laugh. In a biography written by an adoring relative, this description is given: "Laughter and play he considered affronts to the Lord; he hated them, and often condemned both himself and others for occasional lapses into joviality."[6] These representative sobersides of church history believed that laughter was a product of the devil's workshop and thus they attempted to exorcise humor from religion. As a result, being pious has come to imply being solemn. Clergymen are associated with *grave* situations in more than one sense.

Because of this prevailing outlook, Jesus has been caricatured through most of church tradition as long-faced and grim. It is a rare artist who has painted him with a smiling face. Recently, in an extensive survey of the attitudes of Lutherans in America, it was found that most members of that denomination believe that Jesus never told a joke.[7] Friedrich Nietzsche assumed that the image of a somber Jesus was correct and then he used that alleged characteristic as one reason for rejecting Jesus as a personification of the "higher man" *(Übermensch)*. According to Nietzsche, Jesus "knew only tears and the melancholy of the Hebrews." If Jesus had lived longer and had separated himself from those judged to be righteous in his community, then, Nietzsche speculates, "perhaps he would have learned to live and to love the earth—and laughter too!" Nietzsche's Zarathustra supplies what Jesus was thought to have lacked, when he affirms: "Laughter I have pronounced holy; you higher men, learn to laugh!"[8]

Over against this depreciation of humor in church tradition, what was the general Biblical attitude? Abraham, one of the most prominent figures in Hebrew history, doubled over in laughter when told that his old wife was pregnant (Gen. 17:17). According to several of the psalms, even God laughs. One depicts the Lord as highly amused by the arrogance of political rulers who think that they control human destiny (Ps. 2:4; 37:13; 59:8).

Jesus accepted his culture's appreciation of humor and often used it to remove the harshness from criticism. He tried to get his opponents to laugh at their own absurd actions. The Pharisees were extremely careful about trivial regulations, but they overlooked gigantic evils such as slander and prejudice. In criticizing this, Jesus made a "punny" comment: "You strain out a *kalma* and swallow a *gamla*" (Matt. 23:24). *Kalma* is Aramaic for "gnat" and *gamla* is the word for "camel." This is one of many examples of Jesus indulging in humorous hyperbole. In the Gospels there is little humor of the belly laugh variety, but there are flashes of dry wit often based on wordplay. The most famous pun attributed to Jesus is this: "You are *Petros* (Aramaic, *Kepha*), and on this *petra (kepha)* I will build my church" (Matt. 16:18). It is difficult for those who do not understand the languages of early Christianity to catch the subtle and sometimes untranslatable humor. However, there are at least two scholarly books devoted to Jesus' humor.[9]

Anger can be examined in a parallel manner. Today psychologists tend to encourage the expression of authentic anger, viewing it as the price of honest love. George Bach, who has made anger his speciality, demonstrates that "anger is part of the personality, like the sex drive."[10] He thinks that repressions should be permitted to surface as long as certain safety precautions are taken. Gordon Allport also affirms that anger can be cathartic by releasing tensions which could become dangerous if bottled up.[11] He quotes with approval one of William Blake's simple poems:

> I was angry with my friend;
> I told my wrath, my wrath did end.
> I was angry with my foe;
> I told it not, my wrath did grow.

Looking backward over the centuries, we find few who have appreciated the positive values of anger in Western culture. Pope Gregory the Great and Thomas Aquinas listed it as one of the seven "capital" sins.[12] Religious spokesmen have often advised people to pray it away; etiquette manuals have urged ladies and gentlemen to smile it away.

This outlook has been influenced by Stoicism, the chief rival ethic to early Christianity. The contemporary admonition, "Never loose your cool," could well have been their motto. The Roman Stoic Seneca, a contemporary of Jesus, held that anger was "the most hideous emotion" and that not even its slightest signs should be tolerated. He wrote: "To feel anger on behalf of loved ones is the mark of a weak mind." "The wise man will have no anger toward sinners." Seneca illustrates this principle by stating that a good person will not be angry on beholding his father being murdered or his mother being raped. He concludes his long essay on anger thus: "There is no surer proof of greatness than to be in a state where nothing can possibly happen to disturb you."[13]

In the Bible, anger within moderate limits is not considered a vice. Moses so burned with indignation when he beheld his people worshiping the golden calf that he threw down the tablets of law and broke them. But those broken tablets did not contain the commandment, "Thou shalt not be angry!" In Scripture it was not considered unbecoming for even God to be angry, and the usages of the term "anger" are descriptive of divine conduct as frequently as of human conduct.

The Gospels record several instances of Jesus' anger. There is the story of his anger when his disciples tried to keep children from bothering him. As one might expect, he was more often angered by his adversaries than by his friends. One Sabbath, when Jesus was confronted by a sick man, he noticed Pharisees standing around waiting for him to heal the man so they could accuse him of another blue law violation. Jesus was distressed by the callousness of those scornful and unmerciful men. Mark reports: "He looked at them with anger, grieving at their hardness of heart" (Mark 3:5). Jesus was irritated by members of the religious establishment who had more concern for their petty rules than for persons in need.

There are other occasions of Jesus' outbursts at the hypocrisy of the leading religious parties in Palestine. When he saw agents of the priests huckstering at the Temple, he did not fold his hands and pray for patience. Rather he took a whip and drove out the crooked money changers. Jesus thought there were some situations in which it would be immoral to stay calm.

WORK AND LEISURE

There was a rhythm of labor and leisure in Jesus' life. His re-creation seems to have consisted largely of withdrawing occasionally to the hills or to the sea where his frayed nerves and fatigued body could be restored. The Galilean phase of his teaching and healing ministry was interspersed with periods of relaxation for himself and for his disciples (Mark 3:7, 13; 6:30; 9:2). Their holidays were days of psychosomatic holiness and holism, as the root meaning of the two words suggests.

Jesus was critical of those who thought that they must accumulate an enormous surplus of goods before finding good in relaxation. In Luke's Gospel, the "rich fool," who was obsessed with building bigger silos to store his bumper crops, is unfavorably compared with carefree birds who "have neither storehouse nor barn" (Luke 12:16–24). Jesus had little respect for the vast treasures that King Solomon was reputed to have accumulated. For him the wild flowers were more splendidly clothed than that Hebrew Croesus in his dazzling robes. Jesus believed that the lilies, like grass and all organisms, were only temporarily alive but that they nevertheless had a grander beauty than the permanent gleam of Solomon's gold. Hence, for him leisure consisted in separating himself from man's vulgar expressions of self-sufficiency and sensing the throb of uncorrupted nature.

Jesus viewed the world with the eyes of a child in a manner not unlike some modern Romantic poets. William Blake had this aim:

> To see a World in a Grain of Sand
> And a Heaven in a Wild Flower,
> Hold Infinity in the palm of your hand
> And Eternity in an hour.[14]

Alfred Lord Tennyson's earth was also crammed with heaven. He reflected on a flower plucked from a crannied wall:

> Little flower—but *if* I could understand
> What you are, root and all, and all in all,
> I should know what God and man is.

Nature was sacramental with all these men: the fragrant and fragile wild flower was a visible expression of the divine. Theodore Roszak finds in this approach a much-needed corrective to our technocratic "wasteland." With some passion he writes: "Until we find our way once more to the experience of transcendence, until we feel the life within us and the nature about us as sacred, there will seem to us no 'realistic' future other than more of the same: single vision and artificial environment forever and ever, amen."[15]

Jesus' sense of wonder extended to a variety of out-of-door experiences. He was intrigued by grain being reaped, sheep wandering from the fold, sparrows in the marketplace, vineyards being pruned, wind blowing where it wills, and by the sky's ruddy evening glow. Like the bridegroom of the Song of Songs (ch. 2:12–14), Jesus appreciated the flowers, doves, and fig trees of the Palestinian countryside. With respect to nature, his testimony was similar to that recorded in his Scriptures:

> Three things are too wonderful
>   for me to understand—no, four!
> How a bird soars in the sky,
> How a snake crawls over a rock,

> How a ship sails on the sea,
> And how a man loves a woman.
> (Prov. 30:18–19)

These commonplace experiences confirmed for Jesus the psalmist's affirmation, "The earth is the Lord's and the fullness thereof."

According to Matthew, Jesus addressed the divine as "Father, Lord of heaven and earth." Because of this mode of expression and general outlook, Henry Thoreau may have thought of Jesus as "the seer" when he wrote: "When the common man looks into the sky, which he has not so much profaned, he thinks it less gross than the earth, and with reverence speaks of 'the Heavens,' but the seer will in the same sense speak of 'the Earths' and his Father who is in them." Thoreau, who also withdrew to a quiet lake for psychosomatic restoration, believed that man "needs not only to be spiritualized, but naturalized on the soil of earth. We need pray for no higher heaven than the pure senses can furnish, a *purely* sensuous life. Our present senses are but the rudiments of what they are destined to become. We are comparatively deaf and dumb and blind, and without smell or taste or feeling."[16]

Jesus' leisure was devoted to more than the appreciation of nature. From his thorough knowledge of Scripture it would appear that he spent considerable time with it during his two decades of employment as a carpenter. After his baptism, when he went into wilderness seclusion to reflect on his new career as God's spokesman, he wrestled with Scriptural interpretation. At other times Jesus found enjoyment in conversations—as when he talked with Mary before dinner. He criticized Martha, who was so anxious about housekeeping details that she could not appreciate her sister's concern for leisure to engage in dialogue with a rabbi.

Biblical interpreters generally neglect to point out that during his years as a wandering teacher, Jesus was a man of leisure who did not work to sustain himself. He was free to do as he chose. In fact, Jesus was not gainfully employed during the period from his baptism to his crucifixion and he enticed other men to leave their trades and travel with him through the country. Prior to his ministry he had been a breadwinner in his role as carpenter, but he permitted others to provide for him while teaching in the villages (cf. Luke 8:1–3).

Why has there been this one-sided treatment of Jesus which suggests that he shared in human duties and pain but not in human delights and pleasures? Max Weber has shown that there has been a strong tendency throughout church history to believe that "not leisure and enjoyment, but only activity serves to increase the glory of God." The medieval monk who placed a high premium on ceaseless labor was succeeded by the "Protestant ascetic" who considers hard work as the *summum bonum* and concomitantly views as his most urgent task "the destruction of spontaneous, impulsive enjoyment."[17] Such a person regards his grueling, sweat-of-the-brow work not as man's punishment but as his principal means for making life respectable. Consequently he associates leisure with idleness and play with debauchery. Leslie Rutledge has shown ways in which Jesus' use of leisure "is contradictory to the persistent American ideal of 'Blessed Drudgery.' America has been proud of her reputation as a land of strenuous, hurried labor. . . . 'Work for the Night is Coming' has been an American marching song for a century."[18]

FEMININITY AND MASCULINITY

Pernicious sexual stereotyping has been widespread in world civilizations. From the ancient era onward attempts have been made to extrapolate a metaphysical dualism from the alleged antithesis between the sexes. Yang, the masculinity principle in Chinese culture, has been related to steadfastness and brightness; yin, the femininity principle, connotes softness and passivity.[19] In Western civilization the Pythagoreans exalted rationality and rectitude by calling them masculine qualities, while expressing disdain for the irrational and crooked by labeling them feminine qualities.[20] Euripides depicted women in one drama as having an inborn bent toward jealousy, and in another, described them as gossips by nature.[21] Jewish theologian Philo of Alexandria wrote: "Man is informed by reason; woman by sensuality."[22]

These androcentric stereotypes still abound in the twentieth century—in scholarly as well as in popular writings. Sigmund Freud declared that by nature women are more prone than men to behave in egocentric, envious, and unjust ways. In a somewhat milder tone, Erich Fromm has asserted that the preponderance of such qualities as thought and discipline in men is balanced by the concentration of receptiveness and endurance in women.[23] Theologian Emil Brunner maintained that

> the biological sexual function in the man and the woman has its exact counterpart in the mental and spiritual nature of both sexes. . . . The man inclines to be objective, the woman to be subjective; the man seeks the new, the woman preserves the old. . . . He has less difficulty than the woman in admitting that he is a sinner. . . . She is far more sexual than the man.[24]

The life of Jesus illustrates how artificial these polarizations of human characteristics are. It is significant that the Gospel writers describe that model of Christian morality as having traits which traditionally have been at least as much associated with females as with males. To show that this is the case, an examination will be made of several.

The tender emotions have customarily been associated with women. The Hebrew word for woman *('ishshah)* is probably derived from an Arabic root meaning "soft, delicate."[25] Also, the word from the Hebrew Scriptures commonly translated "compassion" is drawn from the root *rhm*, which means "womb." Isaiah describes a mother's feelings in this way: "Can a woman forget the infant at her breast, or have no compassion on the child of her womb?" (Isa. 49:15.)

Other world cultures have also made a close tie between women and the virtues of gentleness and pity. In the patriarchal society of ancient China one influential work gave high value to the feminine yin. In the *Tao Te Ching* these sentiments are expressed: "He who knows the masculine but keeps to the feminine . . . dwells in constant virtue." "Grass and trees are supple and delicate when living but hard and stiff when they die; even so the hard and strong are comrades of death while the soft and tender are comrades of life."[26] Correspondingly, Euripides states: "Woman is gifted with a power of moving sympathy."[27] Even misogynist Arthur Schopenhauer believed that "women show more sympathy for the unfortunate than men."[28]

Weeping, a particular expression of the tender feelings, is also primarily associated in Western civilization with the female sex. Aristotle held that "woman is more compassionate than man and more easily moved to tears."[29] The Roman satirist Juvenal claimed that women always have an abundant supply of tears ready, awaiting the command to flow.[30] In Shakespeare's dramas, "to play the woman" means to weep.[31]

By contrast, in the Semitic culture weeping was associated as much with one sex as with the other. Samson's infamous bride, for instance, used her "hydraulic" power to overcome her husband (Judg. 14:17), but frequently patriarchs and other male leaders also wept (e.g., Gen. 23:2; 29:11; 45:15; I Sam. 24:16; II Sam. 12:22; II Kings 20:3; Job 16:16). Jeremiah, the most profuse weeper in the Hebrew Scriptures, expressed himself in this poignant way: "Would that my head were all water, my eyes a fountain of tears; that I might weep day and night for my people's dead!" (Jer. 9:1.)

The New Testament frequently mentions the weeping of bereaved men and women and contains references to weeping for other reasons by Jesus, Peter, Paul, and John (Luke 19:41; Mark 14:72; Phil. 3:13; Rev. 5:4). Jesus is especially noted for his empathetic ministry in the Gospels. The verb "have compassion"—the customary translation of the Greek *splagchnizomai*, meaning "be moved in one's viscera"— is used in the New Testament exclusively with respect to his life and teaching. It refers to the good Samaritan, to the father of the prodigal, and to the yearnings of Jesus in response to those who desired to be taught, fed, or healed (Luke 10:33; 15:20; Mark 6:34; 8:2; 1:41; Matt. 20:34; Luke 7:13). Unlike Julius Caesar, who a century earlier had announced triumphantly, *"Veni, vidi, vici,"* Luke reports that Jesus *came* to Nain, *saw* a widow mourning over the corpse of her only son, and *"had compassion* on her." Elsewhere in the New Testament the noun *splagchna* ("viscera") is used to express the deep affection of another male. Paul wrote to his Philippian friends: "I long for you with the viscera of Christ Jesus" (Phil. 1:8).

Qualities usually classified as feminine are found in Jesus' comments pertaining to mothers and children. His lament over Jerusalem evokes maternal concern for protecting offspring. He exclaimed: "How often have I longed to gather your children around me as a hen gathers her brood under her wings, but you would not let me!" (Luke 13:34.) He also identified with children by announcing that those who are cordial to youngsters are thereby receiving him (Mark 9: 36–37). When the priests were indignant that Jesus was permitting children to shout hosannas, he reminded them of their Scriptures: "Have you never read that text, 'Thou hast made the lips of children and infants vocal with praise'?" (Matt. 21:15–16.)

Lord Chesterfield and the philosopher Schopenhauer have disparagingly asserted that women remain children throughout life.[32] But Jesus advised adults of either sex to "become like children," and he defined true greatness as keeping alive the virtues prominent in the very young (Matt. 18:1–4). Even on the cross he recited a prayer of trust that Jewish children learned to say prior to going to sleep at night.[33]

Submissiveness has also been deemed a feminine characteristic. As Mary Carolyn Davies puts it:

> Women are door-mats and have been—
> The years those mats applaud—
> They keep their men from going in
> With muddy feet to God.[34]

Jesus stated that his mission in life was "not to be waited on but to wait on others" (Mark 10:45), and he illustrated his humble role by washing his disciples' feet (John 13:5). Luke records that Jesus said at that Last Supper, "I am among you as one who serves *(diakonein)*" (Luke 22:27). This Greek verb is used several times in Luke's Gospel to describe women serving men (Luke 4:39; 8:3; 10:40). The washing of men's feet is referred to in Jewish Scriptures as a handmaid's function (cp. I Sam. 25:41).

Serving needy people in responsibilities beyond the home has also been a role more associated with women than with men. Among the qualities that composed an ancient Hebrew's picture of an ideal woman was this: "She is open-handed to the wretched and generous to the poor" (Prov. 31:20). Today it is still the case that there are proportionately more women in the areas of social work and nursing than in most other occupations. In a summary statement regarding the activity of Jesus, Luke records that "he went about doing good

and healing all who were oppressed" (Acts 10:38). Assisting the social
outcasts—prostitutes, beggars, lepers, and the like—was a main
thrust of his mission.

Suffering is not inseparably welded to serving, but in characteriza-
tions given of women the two are often juxtaposed. Longfellow, for
example, muses:

> The life of woman is full of woe,
> Toiling on and on and on,
> With breaking heart, and tearful eyes,
> And silent lips, and in the soul
> The secret longings that arise,
> Which this world never satisfies!
> Some more, some less, but of the whole
> Not one quite happy, no, not one![35]

Terms referring to the travail of childbirth are used metaphorically
throughout the Bible to describe situations of anguish (e.g., Jer.
13:21; Mark 13:8; I Thess. 5:3). According to the Hebrew Scriptures
intense pain was originally and is most notably experienced by the
human species in giving birth (Gen. 3:16). In his sermon at Pen-
tecost, Peter associated a term for birth pangs *(ōdin)* with the death
of Jesus (Acts 2:24). Paul wrote the Galatians that he would be "in
travail *(ōdin)* until Christ be formed" in them (Gal. 4:19). Jesus
warned his disciples that they will have to suffer like a woman in labor
(John 16:21). As the embodiment of the suffering servant ideal of
Isaiah, he believed that suffering was prerequisite to social deliverance. Consequently he told his followers, "The Son of Man must
undergo great sufferings" (Mark 8:31). So it is seen that Jesus exemplifies par excellence the qualities of suffering and serving which
traditionally have been more associated with females than with males.

Those traits commonly thought to be masculine will now be
sketched in relation to the personality of Jesus. Aristotle claimed that
men by nature are more dominant, courageous, persevering, and
rational than women.[36] These stereotypes have been transmitted
rather uncritically down through our civilization until the present
day. "Bold, resolute, and open in conduct" is the definition that
Webster gives for "manly."

Jesus was noted for his leadership, fearless, powerful, and perspicacious. Many were attracted to him by his words and deeds; some even left work, possessions, and home to follow him (cf. Mark 1:16–22). On encountering a storm at sea that frightened seasoned fishermen, Jesus was not worried (Mark 4:35–41). His calmness in this and some other situations was not due to weakness but was the result of keeping his power under control.

Jesus' power was both moral and physical. A clue to his personality is provided by Tennyson's description of Sir Galahad:

> My strength is as the strength of ten,
> Because my heart is pure.

Jesus' manual trade required bodily strength. Since there were no power tools for sawing and drilling, his muscles were likely even more developed than those of carpenters today. When he became an itinerant teacher he warned those who joined his band that they would need to cope with greater hardships than even wild animals encountered (Matt. 8:20). Like a scoutmaster, he took his disciples on a long hike into the Lebanese mountains (Mark 8:27 to 9:8). He had the stamina to denounce continually the hypocrisy of the religious establishment (Matt., ch. 23), and, at the risk of his life, he physically drove out those who were commercializing the Jerusalem Temple (Mark 11:15–19).

In the masculine mystique of ancient Judaism it was assumed that wisdom was principally possessed by men. It was thus in accord with sex role expectations that Jesus, as an outstanding rabbi, should interpret the Scriptures in a fresh manner, provide keen-witted responses to critical questions, and make astute assessments of persons (e.g., Matt. 5:21–48; Mark 2:23 to 3:4; 11:27 to 12:37; 14:26–30; John 4:7–26). He was recognized as one who had an intellectual grasp of his religious traditions and as one who could communicate authoritatively to those who wished to study that heritage. In that day it was thought that no woman had the ability to acquire such a scholarly temperament.

The Liberated Male

By taking a synoptic survey of all of Jesus' traits, it can be seen that he was a liberated man from the standpoint of sexual stereotypes.

Qualities that many cultures have considered feminine or masculine
were harmoniously blended in his life-style. He affectionately took
children in his arms, but he also indignantly took strong-arm methods
to drive out Temple hucksters. He surprised his companions by being
both more "feminine" and more "masculine" than others.

Empirical studies confirm what the Gospels portray about the
malleability of male and female temperaments. They indicate that
the terms "feminine" and "masculine" are used improperly in reference to psychological traits and properly in reference exclusively to
biological differences: genital organs and their functions, voice depth,
body hair, and physique. Of the twenty-three pairs of chromosomes
of the fertilized ovum at conception, only one is determinative as to
sex. This appropriately reflects the ratio of natural differences to
similarities. Margaret Mead, as a result of an anthropological field
study in New Guinea, was persuaded that the "natural sex temperament" that she went out to discover was a fiction. Rather, she found
that the social conditioning of particular cultures determines the
prevailing patterns of traits appropriate to males and females. Consequently, some societies hold stereotypes that are similar to those of
Western civilization; some hold quite different stereotypes. For example, the women of the Tchambuli tribe aggressively organize the
community and initiate coitus, whereas their men are impractical and
emotionally dependent. Mead concluded that "many, if not all, of
the personality traits which we have called masculine or feminine are
as lightly linked to sex as are the clothing, the manners, and the form
of head-dress that a society at a given period assigns to either sex."[37]

If women are more tenderhearted and men more hardheaded this
is best understood as the result of early nurture, not innate nature.
A number of investigations of sex typing have disclosed the subtle
ways by which parents mold stereotypical sex-appropriate behavior
during the first few years of their children's lives.[38] Naomi Weisstein
and Sidney Callahan, after independently reviewing the studies of
psychological differences between men and women, both conclude
that the differences are due to acculturation rather than to genes,
hormones, or brain structures.[39] However, in some societies even the
impact of training may not be very significant with respect to male-
female psychological traits. A test by John Anderson shows that the
average difference between males and females in his sample is only

one tenth as great as the range of differences among those of the same sex.[40]

Those who regard the imitation of Christ as normative should have no anxiety over whether or not they fit into what culture artificially calls "masculine" or feminine" roles. We can internalize the best of the traditional values associated with the opposite sex without being less a member of our own sex. In particular, Jesus sets the male at liberty to express his temperament and talents even though some may ridicule as effeminate his tears, needlework, or the like. For example, in the 1972 presidential campaign Senator Muskie choked back tears over a published false charge pertaining to his wife. Americans, who evidently think a male candidate should be unflappable, were appalled by his honest expression of tender feelings and thought it would be dangerous to entrust our highest office to a man so unstable as to display tears. It was reported that "the moment of weakness left many voters wondering about Muskie's ability to stand up under stress."[41] Our nation preferred the tough and rather uncompassionate politician who began his career by denouncing those who were "soft on communism" and who ended it by fighting dauntlessly to clear his name from scandal.

Sarah Grimke, an early modern feminist, observed that virtuous women in the Bible are not expected to be soft nor are virtuous men expected to be stern. Rather, "both are equally commanded to bring forth the fruits of the Spirit, love, meekness, gentleness, etc."[42] She was alluding to the Galatian letter of Paul, the same letter in which he claimed that "there is neither male nor female, for you are all one in Christ Jesus" (Gal. 3:28). The apostle was, of course, not unmindful of the physical differences between the sexes. He was, at least in this letter, recognizing a moral equality between the sexes and the qualities that they should jointly share. Elsewhere (Col. 3:12) he exhorts Christians to "put on compassion, kindness, humility, gentleness, patience," a cluster of excellences commonly associated in our culture with femininity at its best. Paul might have agreed with this wise judgment of Theodore Roszak:

> There are no masculine and feminine virtues. There are only human virtues. Courage, daring, decisiveness, resourcefulness are good qualities, in women as in men. So, too, are charity, mercy,

tenderness. But ruthlessness, callousness, power lust, domineering self-assertion . . . these are destructive, whether in man or woman.[43]

In his affirmation of sexual equality, Paul may have been alluding to a teaching of Jesus. In the earliest Christian sermon apart from the New Testament it is stated that when Jesus was asked when the Kingdom of God would come, he replied: "When the two become one . . . and the male with the female neither male nor female."[44] This saying was wrongly interpreted by some Gnostics to mean that women would have to acquire male qualities to be saved[45] and by some ascetics to mean that Christians should reject sexual intercourse as shameful.[46] However, the interpretation given in that sermon— which is probably as early and as faithful to Jesus' teachings as some parts of the New Testament—is this: When a brother sees a sister he should not think of her as female, nor she of him as male. It seems that Jesus taught that masculinity and femininity are not significant distinctions in the ideal realm.

Sexist virtues, which are based on culture rather than creation, should be abrogated. But the alternative should not be a unisex sameness that thwarts the maximizing of individual variations. Rather, the liberated male and female have heightened options for temperamental expressions. Like Jesus, they can choose from a broad arc of possible human traits. They can combine into their personality qualities as varied as shedding tears over the plight of the nation's capital on one day, and striking forcefully against corruption on the next.

A paraphrase of a Hindu fable provides an appropriate conclusion to this study of some of Jesus' personality traits. Once an orphaned lion cub was reared by a flock of sheep. He acquired habits of passivity, and even bleated while nibbling grass. One day a mature lion charged in from the forest to attack the sheep. Indignant at finding one of his kind in their midst, he seized the young lion by the scruff and carried him to a pond so that he could see his reflection. Then, after being given raw meat to eat, the cub became so elated that he burst forth in a triumphant roar.[47]

Likewise, "the Lion of the tribe of Judah" (Rev. 5:5) confronts those whose life-styles are insipidly unauthentic because of stunting acculturation and challenges them to see their resemblance to the perfected divine image. It is a call to appreciate the red-blooded life of freedom. According to John's Gospel, Jesus said, "I have come that they might have life in all its fullness" (John 10:10). This more intense life includes humor and anger, the abandonment associated with leisure as well as the commitment of work, and the development of male-female traits that are most in accord with one's natural talents.

4

Sacramental Sexuality

IN OUR CULTURE the profane and the pious unwittingly work together to forge an inseparable link between sin and sex. "Sin" is exploited by the former to advertise a film for the voyeur and to label a perfume for the seductress. Devout Christians often make a similar sin-sex association, even though, on a conscious level, they view the syndrome as contemptible rather than titillating. By relating sex exclusively to the flesh, and the sacred to the spirit, pietists are offended by the juxtaposition of the terms "sacramental" and "sexual". They seem to believe that God consecrates only solemn or painful experiences, and so cannot be associated with the joy of sexual play.

Contemporary Christians who view sex as sordid follow some influential church leaders who thought of the sacred and the sexual as polar concepts. For example, Origen, the preeminent theologian of the third century, believed that cultic and coital activities were opposed. Following some customary taboos of pagan Hellenism, he warned couples that they could not pray efficaciously on their marital bed and that the Eucharist would be defiled if they partook within a day after copulating.[1] In the fifth century, Bishop Timothy of Alexandria stipulated that Christians must abstain in a similar way before participating in the Eucharist.[2]

The notion that worship should be isolated from conjugal relations also became widespread in Latin Christianity.[3] In the seventh century an archbishop of Canterbury ruled that coital abstinence for three nights before receiving the Eucharist was necessary to prevent the Sacrament from being soiled.[4] Also, the catechism of the Council of Trent, which has been given unqualified endorsement by popes for many centuries, states: "The dignity of so great a Sacrament demands that married persons abstain from the marriage debt for some days previous to Communion."[5] In Catholicism marriage has been called a sacrament—mainly because in the Vulgate translation of Eph. 5:32 the "two in one flesh" experience was referred to in this way: *"Sacramentum hoc magnum est."* However, matrimony has been devalued in that church by making lifelong consecrated virginity, as allegedly exemplified by Jesus and his mother, the prototype of perfection.

Protestants, while not saddled with ecclesiastical directives, seem to diminish marital sexuality according to the degree of their devoutness. The Kinsey survey indicates that there is a one-quarter coital rate decline in the marriages of American Protestants who claim to be "religiously active."[6]

The prevailing Biblical outlook on matrimonial intercourse stands in bold relief against the persistent sexophobia of church history. Had it not been regarded as pure, the Hebrew prophets and the apostle Paul would not have used sexual metaphors in their theology: God is the husband of Israel and Christ is the bridegroom of the church. Had the apostle thought sex was dirty, he would not have summed up his discussion of sexual morality in these words: "Your body is the temple of the Holy Spirit . . . so glorify God in your body" (I Cor. 6:19-20). Paul emphasized that God's earthly sanctuary should be principally associated with human interrelations rather than with stone structures.

In rabbinic Judaism, marriage was called *kiddushin,* meaning "sanctification." The Talmud encouraged the devout to begin the Sabbath by reading from the Song of Songs and engaging in the marital act,[7] on the assumption that these practices would stimulate a more joyous disposition for worship. This sacramental interpretation of connubial caressing has continued in Judaism down through the centuries. In a classic work of medieval Jewish mysticism, this direction is given for husbands: "When Sabbath comes, it is incumbent on them to gladden their wives for the sake of the honor of the Heavenly Partner."[8] Jacob Emden, a famous eighteenth-century scholar, contrasted the Gentile outlook on marital relations with that of his community:

> The wise men of the other nations claim that there is disgrace in the sense of touch. This is not the view of our Torah and of its sages. . . . To us the sexual act is worthy, good, and beneficial even to the soul. No other human activity compares with it; when performed with pure and clean intention it is certainly holy. There is nothing impure or defective about it, rather much exaltation.[9]

The sacramental nature of marriage can best be exemplified by comparing marital sexuality to the sacraments that are commonly accepted by all Christians—Baptism and the Eucharist. Augustine's broad definition of a sacrament as a "visible symbol of something sacred"[10] is an excellent way of referring to the conjugal act. Even as the physical elements of water, bread, and wine are outward signs pointing to inward grace, so marital coitus is a tangible and fleshly event symbolizing something invisible and hallowed. In each of these experiences, things from common life that can be seen, smelled, handled, and tasted serve as sensuous stimuli for celebrating unseen realities.

PARALLELS TO BAPTISM AND THE EUCHARIST

What particular analogies can be drawn from the Sacraments instituted by Jesus and marital sexuality? Paul has most trenchantly expressed the meaning that Baptism should have. He wrote: "By baptism we were buried with Christ, and lay dead, in order that, as Christ was raised from the dead in the splendor of the Father, so also we might set our feet upon the new path of life" (Rom. 6:4). Paul believed that Baptism for adults should be a dramatic re-presentation of Jesus' passion and triumph over death. In this rite, immersion symbolizes that the person who recognizes his unworthiness is forgiven, and rising up from the water witnesses to life renewal that comes through internalizing the spirit of Jesus.

The essential features of Paul's theology have been related to marital relations. Anglican Dorothea Krook has reflected:

> Where more intimately, more intensely, more spontaneously, and more universally than in the act of sexual union between a husband

and a wife is this experience relived and re-enacted—the "dying" to the world by a complete giving up of each self to the other, and the "rising" again into life, new-born, replenished, full of life and joy drawn from the divine plentitude itself.[11]

The conjugal act and the baptismal act have a somewhat parallel significance, even though the latter is a once-only initiation ceremony. The Eucharist, which is perennially renewed, affords even closer parallels to the matrimonial union.

In the Eucharist, the Christian shares at frequent intervals in the life of Jesus. The breaking of bread and the sharing of wine at this holy banquet symbolize divine-human fellowship in a graphic manner. The bond established is an unconditional one: for better, for worse. The Last Supper serves as a vivid reminder of Jesus' steadfast love in spite of the unfaithfulness of his companions. The participant recalls the entire sweep of providential history which has effected this intimate relationship. He not only looks backward to the manifestation of Jesus in the past life of the church but also sees in the ceremony a foretaste of an eventual perfect consummation. On that hoped-for day there will be a complete reciprocation of Jesus' utter self-surrender. Then there will no longer be a partial division at the Lord's table due to petty denominational or ethnic arrogance. Moreover, this covenantal comradeship with one another and with the Lord is viewed as an adumbration of the more glorious life after death. The marvel of this enduring dedication of Christ to the church, his body, is not fully analyzable or explicable.

It is transparent that much of this description of the vivifying and integrative communion at the holy table has overtones for understanding the connubial celebration. Yet, since the associations are rarely if ever pointed out, a number of significant parallels will be made explicit.

First a word regarding the vocabulary used by Paul, whose writings contain the earliest mention of the Eucharist. He referred to the intercourse between the church and Christ as a *koinōnia* (I Cor. 10:16), which has commonly been translated as "communion." In Paul's day that term was also "a favorite expression for the marital relationship."[12] Also, Paul borrowed the verb *kollasthai*, "cleave," from the Septuagint, from the account of the sexual union between

Adam and Eve, and applied it to the union between Christians and
Christ (I Cor. 6:16–17). Thus, for the apostle who wrote definitively
about the Eucharist, the church is a macrocosm of the union of
husband and wife.

In both forms of communion, the partaking of material elements
connotes the unity of the whole self. When Jesus said to his disciples,
"This is my body," he meant that he was lovingly giving them his
total psychosomatic self. Likewise, when spouses engage in genital
sexuality they intend it to be a token of compassionate mutual service.
Havelock Ellis, a pioneer in the psychology of sex, has described what
the sexual experience can be to lovers: "They are passing to each
other the sacramental chalice of that wine which imparts the deepest
joy that men and women can know. They are subtly weaving the
invisible cords that bind husband and wife together more truly and
more firmly than the priest of any church."[13] Perhaps Ellis realized
that the presiding clergyman at Roman Catholic and at Protestant
weddings does not actually "tie the knot." Rather, he declares publicly the covenant which the bridal couple have made with each
other. It is essentially a pledge to bear each other's burdens and to
share each other's pleasures.

Communion unification is not like the merging at a confluence of
rivers. When Jesus prayed in the upper room that his followers "be
one," he did not intend to reject the wide personality differences of
his disciples that he had heretofore encouraged. Likewise, when the
"two become one" in matrimony, the individual self of one is not to
be swallowed up in the dominant ego of the other. On the contrary,
there is a glad acceptance of differentiation so that each remains
completely one's self. Indeed, personal identity is not extinguished,
but is made more distinctive. Each participant realizes that his spe-
cialized role enhances the whole corporate unity. Only after this
awareness of individual differences is fully acknowledged and appreciated can an understanding of complementariness occur. The
mutual subordination that promotes self-fulfillment waxes, and the
lonely isolation that causes self-deterioration wanes.

In the Greek New Testament the same verb is used of a husband
who has carnally "known" his wife as of Jesus being "known" at
Emmaus in the breaking of bread (Luke 24:35; cf. Matt. 1:25).[14]

This suggests that both marital coitus and the Eucharist afford participants a means for gaining a deeper psychophysical revelation of one
another. As defense mechanisms are lowered, the authentic character
of each is nakedly exposed. In the parallel celebrations there is an
opening of one's inner sanctum to the other person and a trust that
one's psychical and biological vulnerability will be rewarded by a
fuller common understanding.

There are several other parallels between the holy supper and
sacramental sexuality. First, for both there is a similarity of approach
which adds splendor to the celebration. Jesus began the Last Supper
with a prayer of thanks which has resulted in the ceremony being
named the "Eucharist." It was intended that the mood of participants be one of joyous gratitude to God. Likewise, in the marital act,
spouses give their functions to one another as a thank offering. Paul's
encouragement of Christians to "give thanks in every situation"
implies that an attitude of gratitude should not be overlooked while
reclining in the marital bed, where a large portion of most people's
lives is spent. A Pauline letter commends indulgence in foods and in
marriage in this way: "Everything that God created is good, and
nothing is to be rejected if it is received with thanksgiving" (I Tim.
4:4; cp. I Thess. 5:18).

David Mace, a noted marriage counselor, tells of partners who
customarily engaged in prayer before sexual communion. As they lay
together in loving anticipation, one of them would say: "For what we
are about to receive, may the Lord make us truly thankful." Mace
comments: "In their simple, artless fashion they were making the
fundamental affirmation that sums up the Christian doctrine of human sexuality; a doctrine that is clearly enough stated in the Bible,
but which had been lost for a long time in a bewildering complexity
of theological confusion."[15]

Second, there is an eschatological aspect to marital sexuality: it is
a foretaste of a more perfect manifestation of the Holy Spirit. John
Milton rightly believed that the union of a husband and wife was a
prefiguring of the heavenly realm. Milton's Adam asked Raphael how
intercourse among nonphysical beings transpires. That archangel responded to this curiosity "with a smile that glow'd," explaining:

Let it suffice thee that thou know'st
Us happie, and without Love no happiness.
Whatever pure thou in the body enjoy'st
(And pure thou wert created) we enjoy
In eminence, and obstacle find none
Of membrane, joynt, or limb, exclusive barrs:
Easier than Air with Air, if Spirits embrace,
Total they mix, Union of Pure with Pure
Desiring; nor restrain'd conveyance need
As Flesh to mix with Flesh, or Soul with Soul.[16]

Sharing Milton's hope for a celestial intermixing, Sidney Callahan has mused: "In this life married people can experience through sexuality multidimensioned joy in knowing and loving another; perhaps this exclusive relationship prepares man for an inclusive love and joy in the new life."[17] Callahan recognizes that Jesus excluded marriage for the purpose of propagation from the life after death, but she assumes that in the life to come there will be no transformation of gender into neuter spirits (Luke 20:34–36).

Third, marital intercourse at its best is like the Eucharist in still another way: both are rituals for communicating that transcend words. The ecstatic moments at the height of communing cannot be reduced to warm prose or flaming poetry. As Paul Ricoeur aptly puts it, the sexual relation "mobilizes language, true, but crosses it, jostles it, sublimates it, stupefies it, pulverizes it into a murmur, an invocation."[18] What Paul said about the Spirit groaning to bring together divided creation is apropos of sexual coupling. The apostle claimed that the Spirit conveys with "sighs too deep for words" what human talk cannot adequately articulate (Rom. 8:26). To borrow an image from the Psalter, "deep calls to deep" in the ideal sexual experience.

ABUSE OF THE SACRAMENTS

Attention so far has been given to what *ought* to be the sacramental meaning of Baptism, the Eucharist, and marriage. However, there is often a yawning gap between their ideal purposes and the way they actually function in practice. Again, instructive analogies that can be drawn from these three sacramental events. With regard to Baptism, there is the constant danger that it will degenerate into a manipulative device for gaining some selfish benefits. The water of baptism is viewed by some as a magical fluid which washes away genetic contamination transmitted from Adam. Others think that both God and one's fellow man might regard an unbaptized person as an atheist; consequently, abstaining from the rite would not enhance one's status either in the earthly society or in the heavenly community.

In a similar manner there are some who view marital sexuality as little more than a way of conforming to religious and social sanctions. They believe that God ordained that man should "be fruitful and multiply" and marriage is the only way of providing legitimate offspring. The second-century apologist Athenagoras exemplifies this outlook: he claimed that insemination was the only justification for sexual indulgence.[19]

Actually there is no good reason for believing that either Baptism or marriage is necessary for a person's salvation. Important as these institutions are, they are not the only means through which the Spirit of God becomes immanent within an individual. An unbaptized person—Abraham Lincoln, for example—may display a more genuine Christian outlook than one who has been baptized. A single person may manifest a more healthy and holy sexuality than one who is married. Moreover, a committed couple who "cleave together in one flesh" may be more "joined by God" than two who have obtained a clergyman's blessing and/or a state's license. If the latter are in a situation of permanent estrangement, it is they who are living "in sin." It is ironical that many in our culture who claim to receive their moral norms from the Bible have often regarded cohabitation to be wicked if it is not sanctioned by an official of the church or the state. Actually, neither priest nor state officer performed weddings in the Biblical culture.

Evidence that the Eucharist has also been abused can be found from the earliest record of its observance. Originally there was more than a mere tasting of bread and wine: a full meal was provided at the home of some members. Paul was amazed to learn that at Corinth those gatherings had deteriorated into an affair in which individuals gorged themselves and became intoxicated. Some took more than their share before the others arrived, leaving the latecomers no oppor-

tunity to participate. Because of such practices the intended symbolism of the meal was lost. Indeed, holy fellowship was more broken
than restored by those gatherings. The apostle charged that some
Corinthians were not observing the *Lord's* Supper but were engaging
in a revolting desecration. He urged that they revere the meaning of
the physical elements, discerning that the broken loaf and the crim-
son wine represent Jesus' torn body and bloody sacrifice (I Cor.
11:20–29).

Even as some early Christians viewed the Lord's Supper as an
opportunity to satisfy individual appetites, so a spouse sometimes
attempts to make the enjoyment of his or her own pleasurable sensations an end in itself. When that happens the relationship degener-
ates from "I-Thou" to "I-It." Marital intercourse can become so
distorted that what was intended as a means of celebrating mutual
service already given and recommitment to future united efforts
becomes a kind of legalized prostitution in which each seeks to
exploit the other. The mate is no more cherished as a person of
intrinsic value than is a maid in a brothel. Just as the ingesting of the
elements of the Eucharist may or may not assure that divine-human
communion takes place, so a physical linking of loins may or may not
be *love*-making. The participants' attitudes determine whether it is
merely an outlet for venereal pressure, a messy mechanism for propagation, a wearisome but compulsive routine, or a consecrated symbol
of Christian love.

LOVE INCARNATE

The sacraments of Baptism and the Eucharist have common characteristics with the marital union both in their ideal symbolism and
in their abuse. All are at once plain and exalted, transverbal modes
of communication. A saying of Goethe applies to all: "The highest
cannot be spoken; it can only be acted." Coital coupling can be a
launching pad for a transcendental experience in which understanding of the divine is unveiled. In this regard, Norman Pittenger has
offered this perceptive insight:

> The essence of love is that in its giving and receiving there is
> complete mutuality and complete faithfulness. . . . When that is

found the other to whom one is bound becomes the sacramental
representation and the given occasion for fulfillment with the
Other who is God. . . . Understood in that dimension, controlled
and governed by the desire for genuine fulfillment in God—even
if God is not named as such, but known only as the "third" who
binds the two in one—sexuality is indeed a wonderful and a glorious thing. Human love, not in spite of but because of, not apart
from but in its physical expression in sexual union is a token and
presence in our midst of the divine charity. And love, so known,
has about it the very quality of eternity.[20]

It is shown in the Bible that there is a profound similarity between
the welcome given the King of Glory by the communing Christian
and the opening up of couples to one another in sexual relationship.
In the Song of Songs, the bride is full of anticipation as she dreams
of a glorious king approaching her bed in hopes of feasting on her
"choice fruits" and "wine." She exclaims, "My beloved is knocking!"
"Open to me, my darling," he calls (S. of Songs 5:2). Regarding that
passage, Phyllis Trible comments: "God is not explicitly acknowledged as either present or absent (though eroticism itself may be an
act of worship in the context of grace)."[21] In Revelation, the risen
Christ is pictured as joining with his bride, the church, in a long-
awaited "marriage supper." He approaches the feast in this manner:
"Behold, I stand at the door and knock; if any one hears my voice
and opens the door, I will come in to him and eat with him, and he
with me" (Rev. 3:20; cf. ch. 19:7–9). In neither communion experience does the bridegroom enter uninvited in a rapacious way; rather,
he patiently waits for a spontaneous response to his initiative.

Apart from metaphorical imagery, what might be said regarding
sacramental sexuality vis-à-vis the historical Jesus? In recent years
some students of Christian origins, scholars from diverse religious
traditions, have agreed that Jesus probably married.[22] Assuming this
to have been true, it is altogether likely that his sexual relations
affected his self-consciousness of unity with God. In any human it is
impossible to make a rigid distinction between loving one's spouse
and loving one's God. If Jesus is the source of the Johannine saying,
"I and the Father are one" (John 10:30), it is possible that he viewed
this theological relationship along the lines of his own marriage. Jesus
elsewhere quoted from the "two shall be one" creation story to

articulate his view of marriage. In both cases the "one" would connote not an identity of essences but a unity of purpose.

Lutheran clergyman Richard Langsdale has used his sanctified
imagination in a recent novel to describe the way in which Jesus
integrated sexual intercourse with his vocational experience as a
joiner. During his honeymoon with Mary Magdalene he reflects:

> Long ago and in another place I had watched my father Joseph
> hone and plane and mold the jointure of two olive boards until,
> with nod of perfection gained and satisfied, he closed the jointure
> and bound the olive wood from two parts into one. So here in this
> night I drew this Mary, this handicraft of God, into human join-
> ture with myself, and through the night we honed the union to its
> height and depth and breadth of intended perfection. We two
> became one.

This intimate love of a particular person does not diminish Jesus' love
for others. On the contrary, he acknowledges: "My life with Mary
has turned a new facet of this prism of love into focus."[23] This
enriching experience is similar to that of Shakespeare's Juliet, who
confesses:

> My bounty is as boundless as the sea,
> My love as deep; the more I give to thee,
> The more I have, for both are infinite.[24]

It is not an uncommon experience that the climax of sexual intercourse affords the religiously sensitive individual with assurance of
at-one-ness with a personal deity. Thus Jesus might have been as
aware of the divine Spirit's nearness on a pleasant bed as on a painful
cross. The openness and responsiveness of optimum sexual interchange could have made him acutely conscious that he was "filled
with the fullness of God himself" (Eph. 3:18–19).

This line of speculation—which some may regard as brazen—
blends with the incarnational Christology that theologian Evgenii
Lampert has suggested:

> In sex and sexual experience man grows into the mystery of God-
> manhood. . . . What, then, is the inner significance of the union
> of man and woman in one flesh? There is here enacted above all

the ultimate out-going of man from himself into the waiting depths of being. He descends and plunges into the world "beneath" and "above" himself, into the breath of the morning of creation, into the dawn of being. It is the moment where in awestruck trembling life transcends its limits. . . . It is the mystery of a sudden merging and union into a single indivisible being of flesh and spirit, of heaven and earth, of human and divine love. The divine spirit touches human flesh . . . in the burning moment of erotic ecstasy. We are witnessing to a true *sacrament:* the Spirit of God invades the cosmic element, without ceasing to be Spirit, and the flesh widens into the transcendence of the Spirit, without ceasing to be flesh.[25]

It is unfortunate that Christians have been quick to be morally judgmental with respect to sexual behavior but slow to draw theological interpretations. This tendency is the opposite of Jesus' own: he forgave the sexually promiscuous and compared the life-style of those in his evangelical band to a joyful wedding. Yet some sensitive contemporary writers have found in conjugal relations an analogy for comprehending more adequately the divine-social intercourse of members of the "body of Christ." Catholic theologian Michael Novak has observed:

Marital sexuality has values which the theologians have not yet begun to touch. It unifies the couple; it often restores their spirits and their energies; it heals wounds; it sends out rays of harmony into all the moments of the day; it sets a standard of trust and communion to which they must live up in all their other actions; it nourishes, judges, and expresses their mutual bond.[26]

In that vigorous tribute to marital sexuality, Novak points to qualities that could also be aptly applied to the Eucharist. In another writing he offers this profound reflection:

The mutual revelation of two people to each other gives rise to the most poignant sense of the sacred in our society. . . . In intimacy and tenderness one "transcends" the acquisitive, impersonal human interchange of our society. . . . For many of the young no human experience is more full of awe, joy and holiness than sexual intercourse. It is from this experience, for many, that religious language becomes meaningful again. The honesty, community, and absolute respect for the other which good lovers are led to share takes them beyond the categories of the pragmatic, the rationalistic, and the isolated self.[27]

Some literary men who have struggled to relate the gospel to contemporary life have found connubial happiness to be one of the best avenues for interpreting the divine-human relationship. W. H. Auden concludes his "Christmas oratorio" with these inspired lines:

> He is the Life.
> Love Him in the World of the Flesh;
> And at your marriage all its occasions shall dance for joy.[28]

D. H. Lawrence, in an essay designed to interpret the outlook expressed in his novels, writes:

> The church is established upon the element of *union* in mankind. And the first element of union in the Christian world is the marriage-tie. . . . Perhaps the greatest contribution to the social life made by Christianity is marriage . . . making it a sacrament, a sacrament of man and woman united in sex communion, and never to be separated, except by death . . . making one complete body out of two incomplete ones, and providing for the complex development of the man's soul and the woman's soul in unison, throughout a life-time.[29]

Lawrence here states the Roman Catholic Church's position that marriage was not a sacrament until Christianity made it such. This is contrary to the Protestant belief that marriage has been sacramental throughout history and in every culture. Seward Hiltner writes: "The Reformers believed . . . that sex and marriage were sacramental in the sense that this realm of life, like other realms, might reveal the majesty and goodness of God through the things of common human experience."[30] Martin Luther found no Biblical basis for the assumption that marriage was a special rite of the church and that a priest's blessing was needed to effect its holiness. He wrote:

> There has been such a thing as marriage itself ever since the beginning of the world, and it also exists among unbelievers to the present day. Therefore no grounds exist on which it can validly be called a sacrament of the new law, and a function solely of the

church. The marriages of our ancestors were no less sacred than
our own, nor are the marriages of unbelievers less real than those
of believers.[31]

The Protestant Reformers may have been influenced by the Brethren of the Free Spirit. That sect was condemned as heretical by the
Inquisition because of its belief that sexual relations have been sacramental from the time of the creation of the first human partners
onward and that coitus is the equal of prayer as a means of experiencing the presence of God.[32]

When the first couple said to one another, "Take, this is my body,"
and when they became "one flesh," they were celebrating the first
sacrament. This does not so much make secular a religious ordinance
as it incorporates into religious mysticism one of the most satisfying
of human relationships. Abraham Maslow's judgment is right: "If we
insist on calling the peak-experience a religious experience, then we
must say that religious experiences can be produced by sexual love.
. . ."[33] In a recent random survey of some 1,500 Americans, Andrew
Greeley and William McCready found 8 percent to claim that they
have had at least one profound spiritual experience that was occa-
sioned by sexual intercourse but "was categorically different from
orgasmic pleasure and much more powerful."[34] This study suggests
that the interpersonal fusion of marital sexuality has triggered for
many millions of Americans an awe-inspiring disclosure of the
"breadth and length and height and depth of love" to which the New
Testament refers.

Love, the *sine qua non* of sacramental sexuality, is the alpha and
omega of Biblical religion. The chapters that follow will trace the
various manifestations of intimate sensuousness from its historical
beginning in the Israelite's community to its eschatological end in the
Christian's Paradise.

5

Agapē Revisited

FROM THE STANDPOINT of breadth of usage, no word in our vocabulary can compete with "love." Nearly every writing included in *Great Books of the Western World* has something significant to say about it. Mortimer Adler, an editor of that fifty-four-volume work, lists love among the five most-discussed ideas of our civilization.[1] Those books range over several thousand years, from the mythical epics of the ancient Greeks to the scientific treatises of the modern Westerner. In the present, as in the past, love is a "many-splendored thing." Readers talk of the books they love. Sweethearts fall in love. Children love peanut butter. Youthful demonstrators have chanted: "Make love, not war." Patriots sing: "God bless America, land that I love." Jews and Christians speak of loving God and neighbors. The elderly chat about the friends and grandchildren whom they love. Some spouses write about their partners as Elizabeth Browning did: "How do I love thee? Let me count the ways. . . ."[2] Looking toward the future, Alvin Toffler states that "the pursuit of love through family life has become, for many, the very purpose of life itself."[3]

Although love has an immense richness of meaning in ordinary usage, it has been uncritically assumed in Biblical exegesis, doctrinal theology, and ethical studies that the Bible's main word for "love," *agapē* (or *agapan*, verb), had an almost exclusively nonaffectional connotation. In a quest for semantic precision, attempts have been made to narrow the concept of love to manageable dimensions. Scholars generally maintain that the translators and authors of the

Greek Bible selected *agapē* in order to avoid the sensual association that was connoted by the Greek noun *erōs*. Catholic theologian Ceslaus Spicq, in his voluminous *Agape in the New Testament*, claims that *agapē* is "completely different" in meaning from erotic love.[4] Karl Barth has declared that there is an "antithesis" between *agapē* and every other type of love.[5] Denis de Rougemont, in his acclaimed *Love in the Western World*, divorces *agapē* from the emotions.[6] Liberal theologian Willard Sperry has asserted that *agapē* and sexual love have "no connection whatever."[7] Conservative theologian Pieter de Jong claims that the apostles "selected *agapē* to express Christian love for each other and for God in order not to confuse this special type of love with sexual love."[8] In an influential essay entitled "Love Is Not Liking," ethicist Joseph Fletcher states unequivocally that to love Christianly is not a matter of feeling.[9] Classicist Thomas Gould holds that for the Christian libidinous desire "is inconceivably remote from the love which is the key to everything."[10] Definitions given *agapē* in Biblical dictionaries and lexicons characteristically assume a sharp difference in meaning between *agapē* and *erōs*.[11]

All these treatments have been influenced by the monograph *Agape and Eros*, by Anders Nygren. He contended that *agapē* is opposed to all kinds of natural human love. Whereas human love is egocentric and possessive, Christian love "has nothing to do with desire and longing."[12] With respect to the ancient Jewish outlook on love, Nygren starkly declared: "What Judaism affirmed, Christianity must deny."[13] Marcion-like, Nygren treats *agapē* as though it were without Jewish parentage, miraculously descending from above to inaugurate the Christian era. In the four decades since *Agape and Eros* was first published he has not altered his position.[14]

The Greek Bible does not support the common assumption that *agapē* should be defined in a way that stands in contrast to ordinary human love. That Bible, following the Hebrew, has no word for sexual love as differentiated from other kinds of love. Consequently, the sensuousness of *agapē* percolates through the most exalted aspects of Biblical man's covenantal bonds. *Agapē*, or its cognates, is used hundreds of times in the Septuagint to express the whole spectrum of human relationships. That translation is the principal quarry from which the vocabulary of the New Testament was mined.[15] In the case of the noun *agapē* this is especially true, for there are only a few instances of its use in extra-Biblical literature.

In Jewish Scripture

The wide latitude of meaning of *agapē* in the Septuagint can best be displayed by reviewing some representative usages. It was frequently used to refer to intimate relationships between individuals. The yearning of an unmarried man for a maiden was called *agapē*. Jacob was willing to work seven years for a woman because of that urge. Cupid's arrow struck him so deeply that those years seemed like only a few days because of the love *(agapē)* he had for Rachel (Gen. 29:20). *Agapē* also drove Amnon to devise a scheme for seducing Tamar (II Sam. 13:1). But the word was most frequently used to refer to affection displayed by the married. In the patriarchal saga it is written that Isaac "took Rebekah, and she became his wife; and he loved *(agapan)* her" (Gen. 24:67). Lest one think that his love was nonsensual, it is stated that he was observed later in life fondling Rebekah (Gen. 26:8). In Ecclesiastes a man is advised to "enjoy life with the wife whom you love *(agapan)*" (Eccl. 9:9). It was assumed that the passionate relationship was mutual. In the Song of Songs a bride testifies: "I found him whom I love *(agapan)*. I held him, and would not let him go" (S. of Songs 3:4). That love song advances the notion that warmth in physical relations can help make marriage permanent. The Song concludes with this affirmation:

> Love *(agapē)* is strong as death
>
> .   .   .   .
>
> Many waters cannot quench love *(agapē)*
> Neither can floods drown it.
>> (S. of Songs 8:6–7)

The noun *agapē*, which always has a sensuous connotation in the Song, occurs more frequently in that book than in all the rest of the Old Testament.

Agapē could also refer to friendships between those of the same sex. David composed this elegy for his slain comrade Jonathan:

> Your love *(agapē)* to me was wonderful,
> Passing the love *(agapē)* of women.
>> (II Sam. 1:26; cp. I Sam. 18:3)

In addition to relationships between individuals, *agapē* connoted goodwill generally. The basic moral law in the Torah is: "You shall love *(agapan)* your neighbor as yourself." Also the passage where that nugget is embedded records an even more remarkable gem: "The resident alien shall be to you as the native among you, and you shall love *(agapan)* him as yourself" (Lev. 19:18, 34).

Although *agapē* primarily referred to interpersonal relationships, there was a secondary impersonal usage. Isaac loved *(agapan)* a certain kind of meat (Gen. 27:4). In the book of Proverbs, criticism is directed toward those who love *(agapan)* sleep and wine (Prov. 20:13; 21:17).

Love was so highly valued among the Hebrews that it is not surprising that they extrapolated love to be the prime attribute of the God they worshiped. They believed that both individuals and groups could be recipients of divine love. In one crisp proverb a theological analogy is drawn from parental correction: "The Lord disciplines him whom he loves *(agapan)*, as a father the son in whom he delights" (Prov. 3:12).

The Hebrews frequently thought of God's love for his covenant community. Hosea was the first to focus on the quality of the love of God for Israel. That prophet probably arrived at his insight by reflecting on his own domestic tragedy. Hosea had married a wife who became unfaithful. Yet he had affection for her in spite of her adulterous conduct and took her back into his home. The prophet realized that in a parallel manner God continued to be devoted to Israel even though his people were guilty of sacrificing to Baal. Hosea's insight is expressed thus: "The Lord said to me, 'Go again, love *(agapan)* a woman who is beloved of a paramour and is an adulteress; even as the Lord loves *(agapan)* the people of Israel'" (Hos. 3:1). Later Jeremiah developed Hosea's theme and proclaimed in the name of the Lord:

> I have loved you with an everlasting love *(agapē)*;
> Therefore I have continued my faithfulness to you.
>> (Jer. 31:3)

Appropriately, the Hebrews worked out the implications of this divine loyalty. In what came to be a part of the fundamental Jewish creed, this moral obligation is affirmed: "You shall love *(agapan)* the Lord your God with all your heart, and with all your soul, and with all your might" (Deut. 6:5).

The ancient Jews did not usually think of God's love as reaching out beyond Israel. Only the Second Isaiah spoke of God's love for non-Israelites. He declared that God loved *(agapan)* Cyrus, the Persian king (Isa. 48:14). That prophet saw that Israel's mission was to carry knowledge of this one true God to all nations (Isa. 49:6).

The Jews who returned from Babylonian captivity did not appreciate the breadth of the Second Isaiah's vision of God's love. From the time of Ezra onward the postexilic community turned in upon themselves. The narrow exclusiveness that developed can be illustrated by an invidious comparison made in Malachi. This oracle is given against Esau's descendants: "I have loved *(agapan)* Jacob but I have hated Esau" (Mal. 1:2, 3).

IN THE NEW TESTAMENT

In Jesus' day it was a common assumption that God loved the Jews exclusively and detested the Gentiles. An apocalypse written during Jesus' lifetime expressed this sentiment: "The Heavenly One . . . will go forth from his holy habitation with indignation and wrath on account of his sons. . . . He will appear to punish the Gentiles."[16] By perverting the Mosaic Code, the Essene Jews formulated these imperatives: "Love all the children of light; . . . hate all the children of darkness."[17] The Mishnah records this inhumane injunction: "The daughter of an Israelite may not assist a Gentile woman in childbirth since she would be assisting to bring to birth a child for idolatry."[18] Many Jews in the first century of the Christian era were militant nationalists. They believed that widespread contempt for the Roman army of occupation would result in a successful insurrection, restoring independence to the Jewish state. Rabbi Joseph Klausner has written: "The Judaism of that time . . . had no other aim than to save the tiny nation."[19]

It was in the midst of such turbulent political currents that Jesus conducted his public ministry. He was perturbed by the rancorous hatred of his fellow countrymen toward foreigners as well as by the animosity among groups and individuals within his own culture. Consequently he aimed at cultivating the concept of love which the authors of Jewish Scriptures had implanted. On the horizontal plane this was effected by his gracious assistance to suffering people. On the vertical plane, he advocated that the one God of all people be loved unconditionally.

Luke's account of Jesus' teaching in the Nazareth synagogue illustrates the way in which his Gospel revived the motif of God's universal love implicit in the teachings of the great Hebrew prophets. After Jesus read from Second Isaiah about the moral imperatives that the Messiah would accept, he cited two episodes about foreigners who were helped by former prophets. Elijah traveled to a foreign city and assisted a widow, even though he could have expended all his efforts on those of his own culture in similar need. Likewise Elisha assisted in restoring the health of a Syrian general. Then, as in recent years, citizens of Israel considered Syria to be a major enemy. These examples show that Jesus thought of God's love as a centrifugal force, ever enlarging the community of those made in his image. But those gathered in that synagogue were infuriated by his insight into Scripture. They could not stomach the notion that God loved all people equally, so they attempted to lynch him (Luke 4:16–30). Although the religious establishment did not succeed in disposing of Jesus that day, at a later date other compatriots, similarly provoked, persuaded Pilate to allow his execution.

Jesus was also concerned with widening the scope of neighbor love within the Palestinian culture. In one of his parables he countered the prejudice against Samaritans. Jesus showed that love is a caring that leads to long-term sharing, and that a member of a scorned ethnic group could manifest it. The good Samaritan's viewpoint toward the Jew is well expressed by Edwin Markham:

> He drew a circle that shut me out—
> Heretic, rebel, a thing to flout.
> But Love and I had the wit to win:
> We drew a circle that took him in![20]

By actions as well as by teachings Jesus mirrored God's steadfast love for all people. He accepted the disreputable: the neurotics and the psychotics, the lepers and the beggars, the tax collectors and the thieves, the prostitutes and the adulterers. This empathy has been expressed in the flaming poetry of Walt Whitman. His Christ figure feels compassionately involved in episodes of human frailty on the realization that "there but for the grace of God go I." Whitman writes:

> Lusts and wickedness are acceptable to me,
> I walk with delinquents with passionate love,
> I feel I am one of them—I belong to those convicts
>   and prostitutes myself,
> And henceforth I will not deny them—for how can I
>   deny myself?[21]

Jesus also prayed for those crucifying him, "Father, forgive them, for they know not what they do" (Luke 23:34). That amnesty petition is an enfleshment of his teaching, "Love *(agapan)* your enemies and pray for those who persecute you" (Matt. 5:44). Jewish scholar David Flusser cites that injunction as the "definitive characteristic" of Jesus' ethic.[22] No Jew living before him had been quite so bold in expanding the concept of neighbor to include enemies. He carried out that radical love in practice by praising the religious concern of a centurion, a member of the foreign army that had humiliated the proud Jewish people by conquering their homeland (Luke 7:1–9).

The earliest interpreters of Jesus saw no discontinuity between the quality of his love for outsiders and for intimates. In the New Testament, as in the Septuagint, *agapē* was such a comprehensive term that it was employed to refer to physical and/or spiritual relationships.[23] Benjamin Warfield, in a thorough and honest treatment of the New Testament terminology for "love" published more than half a century ago, made the following observation:

> The highly preponderating use of *agapan, agape,* in the New Testament is not due primarily to the deliberate selection of these terms by the writers of the New Testament as the fittest to express the high idea of love to which they had to give expression. . . . It is due primarily to the currency of these terms in the Greek native to the New Testament writers as the general terms for love.

. . . There can be little doubt that, had the New Testament writers had occasion to speak at large of sexual love—to write, e.g. a series of narratives like those of Gen. 24 and Judg. 16 and 1 Sam. 13— they would have employed *agapan* and *agape* in them just as the writers of the Septuagint had done.[24]

Robert Joly has recently reinforced Warfield's position by providing further evidence that the usage of *agapan* increased in extra-Biblical texts from the fourth century B.C. onward, and was the common verb for "love" in the era in which the New Testament was written.[25] The fact that the verb is used much more frequently than the noun *agapē* in the Septuagint and in the New Testament shows that the Biblical emphasis was on a dynamic relationship requiring an object rather than on an abstract and static idea.

In spite of frequent claims to the contrary, it is not true that the Biblical writers deliberately avoided using *erōs* and its cognates because it meant sexual desire in pagan literature. Standard classical lexicons show that, in the Greco-Roman culture, *erōs* was also used to connote everything from what is now called erotic to a transcendental relationship with the divine.

Jesus and his apostles found meaningful the variegated ways "love" was used in the Jewish Scriptures. Whether referred to by the Hebrew term *ahabah* (or *aheb*, verb) or by its usual Septuagint translation, *agapē*, it was not for them counter to the normal desire for human fulfillment in marriage or in friendship. To love and be loved, they believed, is a desire shared by God and good humans. Although love is sometimes completely unrequited, usually there is some reciprocation. According to some Gospel parables, even God is not wholly self-abnegating in loving, but finds joy and fulfillment in love that is returned (Luke 15:7, 10). Jesus' ideal person is quite different from Aristotle's "great-souled" person who "is fond of conferring benefits, but ashamed to receive them, because the former is a mark of superiority and the latter of inferiority."[26] Sheer altruism or selflessness was not idealized by Jesus, even though he taught that giving takes priority over receiving in mature love (cf. Luke 6:35; Acts 20:35). The mutuality of love is displayed in the encounter of Jesus with "a woman of the city who was a sinner." She kissed him and wiped his

feet with her hair. He showed his appreciation for the pleasure he had
received by defending her hospitable act and by acknowledging that
"she loved *(agapan)* much" (Luke 7:47). Luke portrays her as more
lovable than Simon, the priggish Pharisee whose home she had entered.

Joseph Haroutunian is properly critical of the common belief that
Jesus' love "flowed out of him as water from a spring . . . unmindful
of any reciprocation." That theologian suggests that those called
"sinners" in the Gospels aroused his affection:

> He saw in them a humanity that escapes the "righteous" and
> is, in fact, repudiated by them. Sinners, like the adultress at Si-
> mon the Pharisee's home or Zacchaeus the publican, for all
> their sins and wrongdoings, showed a sensibility that is the love
> one creature hopes for from another and owes another. . . .
> Jesus not only loved but was also loved in return by the sin-
> ners. It is true that he did not love so that he might be loved
> in return. But it does not follow that he did not care whether
> he was loved or not. . . . Nothing but theological prejudice and
> confusion, accumulated through the centuries . . . would lead a
> man reading the accounts of Jesus' encounter with people to
> judge that his love was a one-way affair.

Haroutunian argues that to be human means to hunger for love and
to feel empty when others do not respond to friendship extended. He
rightly maintains that it is a denial of the humanity of Jesus, and is
thus heretical, to believe that his love was wholly outgoing.[27] Perhaps
Jesus' audacious claim that religious outcasts precede haughty reli-
gionists into the "Kingdom of God" (Matt. 21:31) was based on his
recognition that the former have a stronger concern for mutuality in
love.

FALSE BIFURCATION

Biblical prophets in Hosea's era and later believed that natural love
was not to be renounced but extended. It in no way negates or dilutes
authentic Christian love to recognize that it is continuous with sexual
and family love. Why, then, have Christian theologians been reluc-
tant to relate emotional, sensual love—especially as exchanged be-

tween husband and wife—to the love of God?

The prevailing tendency to impose a dichotomy between divine and human love is due to a distortion of the Biblical outlook which has come through the impact of Greek philosophy on New Testament interpretation. In the *Symposium,* Plato made a sharp differentiation between noble, heavenly love *(ouranios erōs)* and dishonorable, vulgar love *(pandēmos erōs).* The former seeks after clear, rational knowledge; the latter is "of the body rather than of the soul" and is experienced in heterosexual relations. According to that distinguished philosopher, woman has no part in the creation of heavenly love.[28] His aim was to dissociate love from all physical contacts.[29] George Boas has assessed the impact of the *Symposium* in this way: "Probably no other document in European literature has had as much influence on the philosophy of love."[30]

Western philosophers have carried forward the view that true love is independent of emotional expression. What rationalist Aristotle describes as the highest type of love *(philia)* is quite cool in emotional temperature. Philosopher Richard Taylor states: "Aristotle never confuses love with the sexual passion, or *eros.* . . . Few of the ancients thought of it as having any essential connection with love and friendship. In this I think the ancients were basically right."[31] The Stoics held that "the passion of love is a craving from which good men are free."[32] Plotinus, the most prominent non-Christian Platonist, distinguished between the pure form of love that seeks absolute beauty and the vile form that is associated with marital sexuality.[33] José Ortega y Gasset also attempted to lift the concept of love above the common expressions. He wrote in this Platonic manner: " 'Passion' is a pathological state. . . . Love can be . . . clearly distinguished from . . . sensual ardor."[34]

The concept of love often championed in the history of Christian thought has less in common with the Biblical outlook than with the pagan philosophers of the classical era. For example, Augustine of Hippo gave Plato's two forms of love a Latin expression by distinguishing divine love *(caritas)* from cupid love *(cupiditas)* and by calling the latter the root of all evil.[35] In a similar way Søren Kierkegaard held that *agapē* is totally removed from common human affections. He asserted that there is not "one single word" in the New

Testament commending "earthly love." Even more rashly he stated: "If anyone thinks that a man by falling in love . . . has learned to know the Christian love, then he is seriously mistaken."[36]

Throughout church history few have been as bold as the apostle Paul, who used the same term to refer to tender human affections as well as to divine-human ties. He counseled: "Husbands love *(agapan)* your wives as Christ loved the church" (Eph. 5:25; cp. Col. 3:19). William Lillie, a specialist in New Testament ethics, has accurately stated:

> Christian thought has been reluctant to relate our human love between the sexes to the *agape* of God . . . a love that finds its greatest opportunities for self-giving, for its forgiving, and for its richest emotional warmth in the personal encounters of human life —and most of all in the most intimate of human encounters, that of husband and wife.[37]

There are some current studies of Christian love that are in accord with the Biblical outlook. Paul Tillich rejects the assumption that there are different basic types of love and asserts, "Love is one and the various qualities should not be isolated and made antagonistic."[38] William Cole has made a similar point: "The love of God . . . is not some vague, ghostly quality, totally removed from human experience, unlike the love of man for woman."[39] Moreover, George Thomas writes:

> Sexual love and family love, both forms of natural love, are not negated but fulfilled when they are taken up into the life of Christian love. . . . The spiritual life consisting of love of God and love of neighbor is not something that can grow only by renouncing all the natural joys of ordinary human existence. It transforms rather than destroys the affections of our animal and social existence.[40]

In contrast to the polarities that some philosophers and theologians have imposed on *agapē* and *erōs*, the ancient Jews did not attempt to separate neatly the sacred from the profane. The Hebrew term *ahabah* and the Greek term *agapē* are like the English term "love" in that they were used to apply to everything from a sensualist's carnal appetite to a martyr's courageous self-sacrifice. This kaleidoscopic ambiguity discloses love's fathomless meaning. Yet, those with Dante's mystic vision have claimed that the many expressions are but varied pages "bound up in one volume."[41]

Love is the central concept of Christianity as well as the most powerful of human impulses. The quintessence of Christian ethics is expressed in these words of Jesus: "Love *(agapan)* one another even as I have loved *(agapan)* you" (John 13:34). If that "new commandment" is to be taken as a serious obligation and not as sentimental twaddle, the sharp lines of demarcation between the horizontal and the vertical dimensions of love should be erased. *Agapē* should not be torn away from its wide range of meanings in the Greek Bible of early Christianity. Jesus followed the Jewish practice of using the human family as the model for teachings about the heavenly Father (e.g., Ps. 103:13; Isa. 49:15; Luke 11:11–13). The ancient Jews saw the wider community of God as an expansion of the personal encounters in the home. *Agapē*, like charity, begins at home. Emily Dickinson puts this sentiment finely:

> Who has not found the heaven below
> Will fail of it above.
> God's residence is next to mine,
> His furniture is love.[42]

Twentieth-century Christian theologians and journeyman preachers have tended to follow in sheeplike fashion the traditional false bifurcation of the Biblical concept of love that has dominated Christian ethics since Augustine. It is flabbergasting to note how glibly they view the concept through the distorting lens of that bellwether bishop rather than make an independent exegesis of a key concept of the Bible. Luther, trained as an Augustinian monk, carried forward the notion that human natural inclinations are antithetical to the realm of divine grace.[43] Kierkegaard and Nygren, both Lutherans, attempted to impose a radical differentiation between divine and human love on the interpretation of Scripture. However, in an effort to accentuate the significance of Christianity, they have twisted beyond recognition the authentic meaning of *agapē*. Nygren's juxtaposition of *agapē* and *erōs* is not only without linguistic foundation, in the Greek Bible and in other ancient Greek literature, but it is also psychologically absurd. By cutting off *agapē* from down-to-earth love, he tended to present a disembodied religion suitable only for blood-less saints.

Reinhold Niebuhr, in one of his last articles before death, puzzled over the "mystery that the Christian faith is consistently embarrassed by all efforts to relate love to eros." "The sexual impulse may," he admitted, "become the perverse center of human activity, as is attested to by modern pornography, sexual promiscuity and all manner of sexual perversion. On the other hand, it may become the sacrament of love between man and wife." Niebuhr urged that sensual love be thought of as "a seed pod of a more universal love."[44]

Niebuhr well articulates the position of prophetic religion that Nygren and his followers have obscured by their theological propaganda. According to Matthew, neighbor love is "like unto" divine love. To paraphrase a saying from that Gospel: As we engage in love with spouse, family relations, and with persons of all stations in the wider community, we show that we love God with our entire self. (Cf. Matt. 22:39; 25:40.)

6

The Intimate Senses and Beauty

AESTHETICS BEGAN with Plato, who claimed that only the eyes and ears are capable of recognizing beauty. In the earliest extant treatise on the nature of beauty, he argued that smell, taste, and touch can convey pleasant sensations, but not spiritual values. Sexual intercourse, for instance, provides the most pleasant feeling but nevertheless it is "disgraceful and repulsive" and ought to be enjoyed when no spectators are present.[1]

Leading theologians and philosophers have generally accepted Plato's outlook on the beautiful. Consequently Western aesthetics has usually treated only what is experienced by the visual and auditory senses.[2] Augustine held that the senses of touch, taste, and smell are inferior because they "have contact with the object."[3] The senses of sight and hearing, which deal with more distant objects, can communicate transcendent values, whereas those that are immediate cannot. A cleavage between the ultimate and the intimate can be discerned here. Augustine associated the intimate senses more with the ugly and sinful than with the lovely and pure. Aquinas also affirmed that the beautiful is limited to what is seen and heard. He wrote: "We speak of beautiful sights and beautiful sounds. But in reference to the objects of the other senses, we do not use the expression 'beautiful,' for we do not speak of beautiful tastes, or of beautiful odors."[4] Modern philosophers such as Arthur Schopenhauer and George Santayana treat touch, taste, and smell as the "unesthetic" senses.[5]

In the history of aesthetics there have been a few who have not separated the senses into two categories. They have rejected the notion that only the allegedly higher senses of sight and hearing can convey beauty. The British statesman Edmund Burke and the Italian philosopher Benedetto Croce are two who have claimed that *all* sensible impressions can express the beautiful.[6] Thomas Munro explains that the exclusion of the "lower" senses from art and religion is largely the result of the prejudice of ascetic moralists who accept a radical dualism of spirit and flesh and thereby disapprove of senses that are especially connected with physical pleasures.[7]

The Biblical writers did not treat aesthetics in a philosophical manner, but like men in other simple cultures, they assumed that all the senses could convey knowledge of the ultimate. The apostle Paul recognized the primacy of the eyes and ears without denigrating the other sense organs. He believed that all are necessary for proper human functioning, and he even asserted that God treats with special honor "those parts of the body which are considered ignoble" (I Cor. 12:14–25). In one of his mission areas there was a group that championed these prohibitions: "Handle not, touch not, taste not" (Col. 2:21). Paul denounced them because they debased the intimate senses.

Hebrew awareness of the beauty of nature is not adequately expressed in the English translations of the Bible. After various creative acts in the opening chapter of Scripture, there is repeated some seven times an exclamation which is usually translated, "It was good *(tob)!*" But *tob* had an aesthetic as well as a moral connotation. For example, the term is used to describe the loveliness of such women as Rebekah, Bathsheba, and Vashti (Gen. 24:16; II Sam. 11:2; Esth. 1:11). In the Septuagint, the standard Greek word for "beautiful," *kalos,* is used in Gen., ch. 1, to translate *tob.* English versions would be just as faithful to the original if they utilized in that priestly account of creation the term "beautiful." Astronomical bodies, physical geography, and biological life are all beautiful. The account would climax with these words: "God saw everything that he had made, and behold, it was very beautiful."

A selective examination will now be made of ways in which each of the three intimate senses have been related to aesthetic and other spiritual values, in Judeo-Christian history.

BEAUTIFUL TOUCH

The Yahwist story in Gen., ch. 2, features the creation of separate bodies for the human sexes and their fusion in marriage as the most magnificent of all God's works. This becomes more apparent when one recognizes the similar motifs in that story and in the Song of Songs. The latter is, according to A. M. Dubarle, "a hymn to the very good creation of the beginning."[8] Phyllis Trible shows ways in which "the sensuality of Eden broadens and deepens in the Song."[9] In both, humans and other animals romp in a paradise adorned with trees pleasant to the sight and abounding in fruit. The culminating theme of those garden episodes is the erotic encounter of nude lovers. Each writer is aware of the many-splendored expressions of creation's beauty, but focuses on the beauty of heterosexual companionship. The poet of the Song of Songs devoted himself more to describing the beauty of human bodies than of nonhuman things. He might well have said—to paraphrase a saying of Jesus (Luke 12:27)—that Solomon in his sumptuous palanquin (S. of Songs 3:10) is not arrayed like a woman's breasts. The latter are compared in delicacy to young deer and in lusciousness to grape clusters (S. of Songs 7:3, 8).

The ancient Jews were awed by the beauty that was manifested in the flora and fauna and in other terrestrial and celestial aspects of nature. But they were even more sensitive to its revelation in the bodies of both sexes. Saul, the first Israelite king, was the tallest and most beautiful *(tob)* man in the land. But the Lord, finding Saul's beauty only skin deep, soon rejected him and commanded Samuel to select another king. The prophet was instructed to judge not by physical appearance, since the Lord looks on the heart. However, the Lord seemed to have been susceptible to beauty, for when Jesse's sons passed by, the Lord instructed Samuel to anoint David, about whom nothing is stated except that he was exceedingly handsome! (I Sam. 9:2; 16:7–12.)

The Biblical writers were probably all male, so it is understandable that they should more frequently comment on the beauty of women than of men. One of them fantasized that human women were so beautiful *(tob)* that semidivine beings chose some of them as wives (Gen. 6:2). Abraham's wife is introduced as one so "beautiful to behold" that a Pharaoh took her into his harem (Gen. 12:11–15). A Qumran scroll contains a head-to-foot description of the charms Sarah was imagined to have had. "How radiant her face; how fine the hair of her head; how fair indeed are her eyes; how pleasing her nose, how beautiful her breasts, how lovely all her whiteness; her arms goodly to look upon; her hands how perfect; her legs how beautiful and how without blemish her thighs."[10]

The expressions of beauty that have been considered above are related to the visual as well as to the tactile senses. Of the two there are some who regard the latter as at least as significant as the former. Helen Keller, with her "three trusty guides, touch, smell, and taste," made excursions into aesthetics. She stated:

> In my classification of the senses . . . touch is a great deal the eye's superior. I find that great artists and philosophers agree with me in this. Diderot says: "I found that of the senses, the eye is the most superficial, . . . touch the most profound." . . . Lorenzo Ghiberti, after describing a piece of antique sculpture he saw in Rome adds, . . . "Its more exquisite beauties could not be discovered by the sight, but only by the touch of the hand passed over it."

Keller, in a personal testimony, shows how the skin is, even apart from sexual caressing, a subtle means for discerning loveliness:

> Press the soft blossoms against your cheek, and finger their graces of form, their delicate mutability of shape, their pliancy and freshness. . . . How can the world be shriveled when this most profound, emotional sense, touch, is faithful to its service? I am sure that if a fairy bade me choose between the sense of sight and that of touch, I would not part with the warm, endearing contact of human hands or the wealth of form, the nobility and fullness that press into my palms.[11]

Frances Herring, in an essay entitled "Touch—the Neglected Sense," makes this point: "Aesthetic tactile experiences are among the most *profoundly integrating* of any obtainable through art. Perhaps because it is biologically the oldest sense, out of which the other senses have developed through the long ages, it seems psychologically easiest to achieve a sense of *restoration to simplicity,* of *unity,* through touch."[12]

LOVELY SMELL

The Hebrews valued having well-washed and pleasant-smelling bodies. Consequently their priests associated physical uncleanliness with religious unholiness. In spite of the scarcity of water in Palestine for much of the year, they gave this directive for the man or woman having bodily discharges: "He shall bathe his body in running water" (Lev. 15:13). A Jewish apocalyptic writing from the Biblical era asserts that those who honor God are "ever cleansing their flesh with water." This imperative is given: "Wash your whole bodies in ever-running rivers." It is to the teaching of the Hebrew father Phinehas ben Yair over two millennia ago that the proverb "Cleanliness is next to godliness" has been traced.[13]

According to a midrash, the distinguished rabbi Hillel explained that he washed his body because it was the locus of the King of Kings. He had this conversation with his disciples:

"Where are you going, Hillel?"
"To take a bath."
"Is that a religious act?"
"Yes; if images of the king in public places are kept clean by the custodian how much more is it a duty of man to care for the body, since he has been created in the divine image."[14]

The attitude toward bathing in the Jewish tradition has been in harmony with Hillel's outlook. There was a bathhouse for priests in the temple built by Herod.[15] The Mishnah tells of Rabbi Gamaliel's defense of patronizing a bathhouse at Acre that was graced by a statue of Venus.[16] In spite of the customary antagonism between the Jewish and Roman cultures, the Talmud expresses appreciation for the baths which the Romans constructed in Palestine and prohibits Jews from living in cities which lack public baths.[17] Max Grunwald explains that "the heat and dust of the Orient made frequent bathing a generally popular custom and sanitary requirement of long standing among Jews."[18]

Bathing was usually followed by perfuming the body. The story of the Jewish heroine Judith states that she bathed daily and that before attempting to seduce the Assyrian king she "bathed her body with water and anointed herself with precious perfume" (Judith 10:3; 12:7). Ruth and David anointed themselves after bathing (Ruth 3:3; II Sam. 12:20). There are more than a dozen perfumes named in the Bible[19] and these were used by both men and women (Esth. 2:12; Ps. 45:8; Prov. 7:17). The raw materials for perfumes were roots, sap, bark, leaves, and flowers of certain pungent plants found in widely separated areas of Asia. Throughout history a considerable part of commerce has been associated with conveying from distant places the spices needed by perfumers. Indeed, the geographic discovery of much of the earth has been the result of explorers following their nose in the quest of pleasant fragrances. The exotic spices were combined with vegetable oils in order to make cosmetics that would adhere to the skin. The Song of Songs indicates that they were also placed in the clothing or chewed to sweeten the breath (S. of Songs 1:13; 7:8). That writing is rated by olfactory specialist Roy Bedichek as "the most odorous love poem in all our literature."[20]

Since sweet aromas were enjoyed by ancient Near Eastern peoples, they assumed that it was fitting to give incense to those they desired to honor. Thus it was offered to kings and deities in various cultures (Dan. 2:46). According to Matthew's Gospel, the gifts which the Eastern magi brought for a Jewish ruler were mainly perfumes— frankincense and myrrh. Holy smoke was prominent in Israelite worship and a special recipe for mixing the substances for making this incense is given (Ex. 30:34–38).

In the Bible, God is referred to as sniffing aromas more than man. The best-known episode containing this bold anthropomorphism comes at the conclusion of the flood when Noah offered burnt animal sacrifices on an altar. The account states: "When the Lord smelled the pleasing odor he said within himself, 'Never again will I curse the ground because of man, however evil his inclinations may be from his youth onwards' " (Gen. 8:21). According to both priestly and prophetic literature, divine rejection of hypocritical ceremonies is expressed thus: "I will not smell your pleasing odors" (Lev. 26:31); "I will not smell your solemn assemblies" (Amos 5:21, KJV). In the Pentateuch and in the Psalter, idol gods who "have noses, but do not smell" are invidiously compared to the God of Israel (Ps. 115:6; Deut. 4:28).

The motif of an odor-sensitive deity has been expanded in recent centuries. John Milton compensated for his blindness by giving much attention to scents in his poetry. He provides this theological and aesthetic figure:

> Now when as sacred Light began to dawne
> In *Eden* on the humid Flours, that breathd
> Thir morning incense, when all things that breath,
> From th' Earths great Altar send up silent praise
> To the Creator, and his Nostrils fill
> With gratefull Smell, forth came the human pair. . . .[21]

Helen Keller perceptively noticed that in the symbolism of the Israelite temple, God dwells sightless in "thick darkness" within the Holy of Holies, yet he whiffs the spice incense offered him (I Kings 8:12; II Chron. 2:4). She comments:

> In my experience smell is most important, and I find that there is high authority for the nobility of the sense which we have neglected and disparaged. It is recorded that the Lord commanded that incense be burnt before him continually with a sweet savor.[22]

The general Jewish appreciation for perfumes, incense, and bathing continued to be much in evidence in early Christianity. Perfumes were even more a luxury item then than now but, even so, peasant Jesus encountered a woman at Bethany who poured a jar of costly nard over his head. He welcomed this lovely gesture—extravagant though it was, and even though some who witnessed it were disgusted over the woman's "waste" of wealth. Jesus said, "Let her alone; why do you trouble her? She has done a beautiful thing to me" (Mark 14:3-9). He thus discerned more of beauty in the intimate senses than some of his compatriots—especially the Essenes, who washed ceremonially but rejected the use of anointing oil.[23]

Jesus lived in an era when having one's feet anointed with soothing salve or washed in scented water was regarded as a delightful treatment.[24] He cordially received a woman who wet his feet with a mixture of ointment and tears (Luke 7:37-50). According to John's Gospel, Jesus washed the feet of each of his disciples during the Last Supper (John 13:2-11). The purpose of this action was to symbolize the importance of humble service, but it incidentally showed that he was not unmindful of the advantage of treating feet so that they were neither unpleasant in odor nor pained from walking on the hot and dusty Palestinian roads in crude footwear.

What was later said of Mohammed could also have been said of Jesus: "Perfume he loved passionately, being most sensitive to smells."[25] Carl Sandburg's description might have applied to both of these Semitic prophets: "This Jesus was good to look at, smelled good, listened good. He threw something fresh and beautiful from the skin of the body and the touch of his hands wherever he passed along."[26]

Because of the high value placed on the sense of smell in the Old and New Testaments, perfumes were sometimes given a figurative meaning. An Israelite bride compared her beloved to "myrrh that lies between my breasts" (S. of Songs 1:13). The apostle Paul thought of the gospel in Christians as an aroma that spreads widely, making life more vital to those affected. He wrote: "We are the fragrance of Christ, pleasing to God and diffused among those who are being saved" (II Cor. 2:15). A Hebrew psalmist and a Christian visionary discerned a parallel between incense and prayer rising heavenward. The former made this plea: "Let my prayer be like incense" (Ps. 141:2). The latter described those who surround God's throne: "Each of the elders had a harp, and they held golden bowls full of incense. . . . The smoke of the incense went up before God with the prayers of his people" (Rev. 5:8; 8:4).

The Biblical appreciation of clean and perfumed bodies was reversed with the rise of the monastic movement in the third century. Anthony, the first famous Christian monk, believed that spiritual fiber is strengthened to the extent that pleasures of the body are diminished. A contemporary of his reports that "he would not anoint himself with oil."[27] He was ashamed to see even his own nakedness, so he did not change his clothes. Moreover, "he neither bathed his body with water to free himself from filth, nor did he ever wash his feet."[28] Anthony was followed by Pachomius, who ruled that washing was forbidden in monasteries, except for sick persons.[29]

Jerome believed that cleanliness is far from godliness and that virtue is associated with offensive body odor. He spoke fondly of Paula, who was "squalid with dirt," used no perfumes, and lived by the motto, "A clean body means a dirty mind."[30] "I wholly disap-prove of baths for a virgin who has come of age," Jerome wrote; "such a one should blush and feel overcome at the idea of seeing herself undressed."[31] He advised a monk: "Let your garments be squalid to show that your mind is white. . . . Baths stimulate the senses and must, therefore, be avoided."[32] Ironically it was John, whom Jerome believed was preeminent among the apostles, who was mentioned in early Christian tradition as frequenting the public baths at Ephesus.[33]

Those ascetic Christians who associated giving up bathing with becoming a follower of Jesus had considerable influence in Western culture. Friedrich Nietzsche commented: "In Christianity . . . the body is despised, hygiene repudiated as sensuality; the Church even resists cleanliness (the first measure taken by the Christians after the expulsion of the Moors was the closure of the public baths, of which Cordova alone possessed 270)."[34] While Nietzsche was wrong to assume that the extreme monastic position was normative, the com-plete divorce of pleasant smell from holiness was largely due to those austere men and women. Medieval culture has been hyperbolically described as "a thousand years without a bath." The epidemics of that era were in part due to low standards of hygiene. One of the results of the Crusades was to bring the bath from the Eastern Mediterranean to western Europe.[35]

In modern history there have been a few attempts to revive the ancient indulgence in pleasant aromas and to find in them theological and philosophical meaning. Protestant Reformer John Calvin que-ried: "Has the Lord clothed the flowers with the great beauty that greets our eyes, the sweetness of smell that is wafted upon our nos-trils, and yet will it be unlawful for our eyes to be affected by that beauty, or our sense of smell by the sweetness of the odor? . . . Did he not, in short, render many things attractive to us, apart from their necessary use?"[36] Theodore Roszak laments that contemporary soci-ety has allowed the eyes and ears to predominate while our other senses atrophy. "Most notably," he observes, "the human power of smell, which remains so vibrantly alive in other mammals, degener-ates. . . . Our conscious relations with the world have become almost exclusively those of a spectator looking on and listening in."[37] The widespread use of artificial flowers—colorful but odorless—illustrates the way the more distant sense of sight has been given exclusive priority over the more immediate sense of smell. Herbert Otto has written: "Smell, as one of the most basic and primitive senses, can put man in touch with the very wellsprings of his being and the core of his becoming. Regeneration of our sense of smell can add avenues of communication, deepen the dimensions of our identity, and make us more clearly aware of our at-one-ness with nature."[38]

GOOD TASTE

The saying "Eat, drink, and be merry" is generally associated with hedonists whose life-styles are contrary to the outlook of Christians. It is assumed to have originated with pagan carousers and is frequently attributed to the Epicureans.[39] Because of the monastic tradition in the West it has often been assumed that the Christian attitude has been "Fast, abstain, and be solemn." Anthony, for example, took no meat or wine and consumed only enough bread and water to survive. He was so ashamed of having to satisfy his hunger that he separated from others while eating.[40] Jerome likewise recommended a meatless and wineless diet and believed that virtue increases if the appetite is always unsatisfied.[41] Augustine treated food as medicine and consumed only enough to avoid illness.[42] Francis of Assisi diligently avoided the pleasure of tasty food. When given cooked food he would "either sprinkle it with ashes, or by pouring water thereupon would as far as possible destroy its savor." He not only abstained from wine but drank scarcely enough water to quench his thirst.[43]

Calvin called this asceticism characteristic of the medieval saints "very dangerous" because it tries to "fetter consciences more tightly than does the Word of the Lord."[44] As a corrective he gave this exposition of the story of Joseph's reunion with his brothers:

> There was a sumptuous banquet at which they indulged themselves more freely and hilariously than was usual. . . . If anyone raises the objection that a frugal use of food and drink is sufficient for the nourishment of the body, I answer: although food is a

proper provision for our bodily need, yet the legitimate use of it goes beyond mere sustenance. For good flavors were not added to food value without a purpose, but because our Heavenly Father wishes to give us pleasure with the delicacies he provides. It is not by accident that Psalm 104:15 praises his kindness in creating wine to cheer man's heart.[45]

Calvin accurately interpreted the prevailing Biblical outlook on eating and drinking. Indeed, the saying "Eat, drink, and be merry" is a Biblical expression that is usually used with approval.[46] "Being merry" is customarily associated with feeling the effects of wine (I Sam. 25:36). It might be said that the Hebrews found God's creation to be "finger-lickin' good"!

Jesus regarded feasting rather than fasting as the appropriate expression of his "good news." In contrast to John the Baptist he affirmed that "the Son of man has come eating and drinking" (Luke 7:34). The Gospels amply illustrate that this was indeed the case. New Testament critic Norman Perrin, who has precious little to say about the historical Jesus and his disciples, nevertheless recognizes that "a central feature of the life of this group was eating together, sharing a common meal that celebrated their unity in the new relationship with God."[47]

In the Synoptic Gospels there are episodes related to Jesus eating with "multitudes" and with small groups. He joined a party that Matthew threw for his cronies, and this caused some Pharisees to inquire, "Why do you eat and drink with tax collectors and sinners?" (Matt. 9:10–11; Luke 5:29–30.) His places of eating were quite varied: he invited himself to the home of Zacchaeus the tax collector (Luke 19:5); he also accepted the dinner invitation of Simon the Pharisee (Luke 7:36). Some of the meals of his traveling band were obtained from fruit trees and grainfields along the way, and at least one was prepared in the home of Simon Peter (Mark 1:31; 2:23; 11:12, 13). Several of Jesus' parables pertain to banquet etiquette— who the host should invite and how the guests should behave (e.g., Luke 14:7–24; 16:19–23).

It is significant that one of the best-remembered experiences of Jesus' disciples was associated with a sensuous supper. All five senses were involved when they partook of the Last Supper in Jerusalem.

Those gathered in the "upper room" saw, touched, smelled, and tasted what was on the table, and they heard what Jesus said about the bread and the wine.

Feasting is also prominent in the Fourth Gospel. There Jesus is represented as beginning his ministry by attending a marriage feast. The party probably consisted of the perennial fare for wedding receptions across the ages—giggling, gabbling, gobbling, and guzzling. The Gospel of John concludes with a fish fry on a beach. Jesus prepared a breakfast for his disciples before conversing with them, showing that meals were for him occasions for fellowship as well as for consuming food. Several of the chapters of that Gospel are devoted to table talk associated with the dinner given during the Passover celebration on the night before Jesus' death.

At that Supper, Jesus gave a new commandment to love *(agapan)* one another (John 13:34). It is probably because of that teaching and setting that the early Christians called their affectionate common meal an agape (Jude 12).[48] The customs associated with it were derived from Jewish meal practices.[49] Tertullian defended the practice in this manner: "Our dinner shows its purpose in its name, "love," as it is called by the Greeks. . . . The participants, before reclining, taste first of prayer. As much is eaten as satisfies the cravings of hunger; as much is drunk as befits the modest."[50]

It was the Christian ascetics that caused the agape to be discontinued within the church. Bishop Ambrose prohibited the practice out of fear that some might become intoxicated.[51] His disciple Augustine held that "not even innocent and temperate feasts" should be permitted among Christians. When he was reminded that Christians in the past had this practice, Augustine responded: "Let us now at last put down what ought to have been earlier prohibited."[52] Medieval church councils upheld the ascetics' position by stating: "It is not lawful to hold the so-called agape in the churches, or assemblies, and to eat, or set out couches in the house of God."[53]

After more than a thousand years of neglect, some modern attempts have been made to bring back the agape. The most successful attempt has been that of the Moravians, who in 1727 revived what they call the "love feast." Warmth of fellowship is lubricated by sweet buns and coffee served in their churches.

Largely because of burgeoning technology, the ceremonializing of eating is on the wane. For many, food is little more than a fuel to fill up on at roadside stations, or an "instant" preparation item obtainable from stores. Savory food of ethnic origin has given way to a bland fare that can be quickly consumed and that neither offends nor titillates the palate. Hungry Americans on the go seem to opt for food that slides rapidly under the nose and over the tastebuds without being noticed. Some eat to live in much the same way that married ascetics have indulged in sexual relations: it is little more than a necessary evil for keeping the human species alive. It would be uncanny to hear someone exclaim today with the ancient psalmist: "O taste and see that the Lord is beautiful *(tob)!*" Michael Novak put it this way: *"Homo sapiens* has tried to forget that the root meaning of *sapiens* is 'taste'—biting into a cold apple, a lick of honey. . . ."[54] However, as one who was raised in the Shenandoah Valley of Virginia, this writer has not forgotten the sensuous qualities of its famous fruit! I endorse this tribute:

> For the touch, apples offer a shape that invites you to curl your hand around it. For a visual treat the apple tree offers its beautiful blossoms in spring, the distinctive green of its leaf in summer, the bright contrasts of the fruit-full orchard in fall, the dramatic silhouette of gnarled, bare branches in winter. For the nose: the scent of the blossoms, the fine fall aroma of the fruit. For the palate, tastes from tart to sweet and countless recipes, beginning with pies and cobblers and ranging wide. But best of all, perhaps, is the bite. That first sweet, juicy snap of a Stayman makes a moment to be savored. Thank you, God, for apples.[55]

Conclusion

We have inherited from Plato a bias toward the organ of sight. Western civilization has been greatly influenced by his key word *idea*, which is derived from the verb "to see." He believed that the realm of ideas was the source of beauty and all our other concepts. The ancient Jews appreciated visual beauty but balanced sight with the other senses as an avenue to true knowledge. Aware of the perils of idolatry, they did not principally associate their fine arts with objects that could be seen. They also experienced aesthetic delight in the sound of music and poetry, in the fragrance of perfume and flowers, in the taste of savory food, and in the feel of human bodies. The Song of Songs grandly exemplifies the aesthetic interests of the ancient Jews, for in it all the senses are finely orchestrated. There the bridegroom says:

> The flowers appear on the earth;
> The time of singing has come,
>   and the cooing of the turtledove is heard in the land.
> The fig tree puts forth its figs,
>   and the vines give forth their fragrance.
> Arise, my beautiful love, and come away.
>   (S. of Songs 2:12–13)

The poet-mystic Kahlil Gibran, drawing on his Lebanese background, has contrasted the sensitivity of the creative Jesus with that of the *hoi polloi.* Gibran portrays Jesus in this light:

> He loved all things of loveliness, the shy faces of children, and the myrrh and frankincense from the south. He loved a pomegranate or a cup of wine given him in kindness. . . . In truth we gaze but do not see, and hearken but do not hear; we eat and drink but do not taste. And there lies the difference between Jesus of Nazareth and ourselves. His senses were all continually made new, and the world to him was always a new world. To him the lisping of a babe was not less than the cry of all mankind, while to us it is only lisping. To him the root of a buttercup was a longing towards God, while to us it is naught but a root.[56]

Moderns in pursuit of the sublime have much to learn from those sensuous Jews of the Biblical era. They would have modified our popular saying, "Beauty is in the *eye* of the beholder." We are becoming vulturelike in our dependence on the eye—on what Wordsworth referred to as "the most despotic of our senses." That poet muses:

> Could I endeavor to unfold the means
> Which Nature studiously employs to thwart
> This tyranny, summons all the senses each
> To counteract the other.[57]

Generally speaking, the ancient Jews resisted overindulging any one sense. They discerned that overindulgence in the senses other than sight could also be idolatrous. For example, Paul summed up the value orientation of some opponents of Christianity with these words: "Their god is the belly" (Phil. 3:19). He recognized that those who attempt to make good food the end of life are flaunting the ethical priorities that make for community. To some who were concerned with the dietary restrictions appropriate to the Christian, the apostle gave this guideline: "Whether you eat or drink, or whatever you do, do all for the glory of God" (I Cor. 10:31). A succulent beefsteak for one's own body should not, he believed, become so glorious that the "body of Christ" is overlooked. Those who grasp the significance of that metaphor place individual tastes in proper perspective. The welfare of other persons in the corporate body, and indeed the total health of one's own body, must be given due consideration. Those who criticized the woman who poured enormously expensive perfume on Jesus had a utilitarian sensitivity that needs always to be weighed before indulging in beautiful experiences. Does the experience, sublime as it might be, deprive others of what they need for a life of happiness and reverence? Or, does it cause an imbalance in one's life so that other personal needs are neglected? There is, in short, an interrelation between what is beautiful and what is morally right.

The challenge of the religious life is to integrate and order priorities so that each person and his neighbors can "glorify God and enjoy him forever." Calvin wrestled with the problem of how to avoid being a gluttonous pig on the one hand and an abstemious prig on the other. The enjoyment principle that he hammered out is profound —even though many of his followers have disregarded his appreciation for beauty derived from the intimate senses. He wrote:

The use of God's gifts is not wrongly directed when it is referred to that end for which the Creator himself made and appointed them for us, since he created them for our benefit, not for our injury. . . . Now if we ponder for what end God created food, we shall find that he meant not only to provide for necessity but also for delight and good cheer. . . . In herbs, trees, and fruits, apart from their various uses, his design has been to gratify us by beauti-

ful forms and pleasant odors. For if this were not true, the Psalmist
would not have recounted among the benefits of God "wine that
makes merry the heart of man, and oil that makes his face shine."
. . . Away, then, with that inhuman philosophy which, allowing no
use of creation except what is absolutely necessary, not only malig-
nantly deprives us of the lawful enjoyment of God's beneficence
but cannot be practiced unless it robs a man of all his senses and
degrades him to a block.[58]

The Jesuits have given considerable attention to the fact that the
raw material of consciousness comes by sense stimili and that hints of
God can come through these varied sensuous sources. Ignatius Loyola,
in his *Spiritual Exercises,* recommended that each sense should be
focused on separately to get the full theological impact. Lawrence
Meredith recently used Loyola's approach during a pre-Easter season
to prepare a college group for the resurrection of the body. Each week
one of the five senses was singled out for celebration. When the focus
was on taste, a rabbi was invited to eat with them and chat about the
religious appreciation of food in the Jewish tradition. This was concluded with the circulation of a goblet of wine. Touch was dealt with
by a blind student who described the texture of common objects to a
blindfolded congregation. On the other occasions a jazz liturgy composer let the group hear and produce some novel sounds, art work was
viewed and discussed, and trays containing objects of different odors
were passed around.[59] Jesuit Teilhard de Chardin gives a theological
context for such sensuous participation when he writes:

> God, in all that is most living and incarnate in him, is not far away
> from us, altogether apart from the world we see, touch, hear, smell,
> and taste about us. . . . What would our spirits be, O God, if they did
> not have the bread of earthly things to nourish them, the wine of
> created beauties to intoxicate them? . . . Let us establish ourselves in
> the divine *milieu.* There we shall find ourselves where the soul is
> most deep and where matter is most dense. There we shall discover,
> where all its beauties flow together, the ultra-vital, the ultra-sensi-
> tive, the ultra-active point of the universe.[60]

In the next chapter detailed consideration will be given to the
liturgical and nonliturgical ways in which one of the intimate senses
has been employed in the Judeo-Christian tradition.

7

The Kiss of Love

TACTILE RESISTANCE is a characteristic of contemporary Western culture. Touching—even by means of a handshake—is engaged in nervously by most Americans, so there is much reluctance to engage in kissing apart from a romantic setting. Men especially are trained to avoid displaying openly tender expressions of acceptance and trust. Ashley Montagu remarks: "There are whole cultures which are characterized by a 'Noli me tangere,' a 'Do not touch me' way of life." "In forty years of close observation I have only once seen an adult American male publicly greet his father with a kiss."[1] Thus we seem to have an unwritten touch-me-not policy that even extends to filial associations.

If we meet a baby kisser and backslapper who wants to "press the flesh"—to use an expression of Lyndon Johnson—we assume that he is a politician. However, Aristotle argued that gregarious or "political" behavior is not a peculiarity but an essential human characteristic. He also held that touch is the most fundamental of the animal senses.[2] While this is generally true of mammals, it is especially true of primates, our closest living relatives. Jane Goodall informs us that chimpanzees communicate by means of "kissing and embracing, touching and patting and holding hands."[3]

Since intimacy is a part of our natural animality, it is culture that makes for social distance. Our patterns for primary group interaction tend to duplicate the necessarily impersonal approach of the public media. Television, radio, telephones, and newspapers can communicate with us only through our eyes and ears. The idiom "Keep in touch" has come to mean little more than an occasional nontactile telephone or eyeball-to-eyeball conversation along with an exchange of letters.

Social scientist Margaret Mead has commented:

It seems to me that the average middle-class American is exceedingly inhibited about touching other people. . . . Now my general experience in working with black people is that I always have to touch them, or they touch me, if we are going to get anywhere. I feel, if I don't touch them, I haven't communicated with them at all. I could sit across the room and make beautiful speeches forever, but one touch makes the difference, just one touch.

Black writer James Baldwin, agreeing with Mead, described his childhood experience in the lower class: "We all grew up on top of each other, slapping each other or kissing each other or whatever. But we always touched each other. . . . Not touching a person is a way of rejecting him."[4]

To describe the dominant mood emerging in our technological culture, psychiatrist Rollo May uses the terms "schizoid" and "apathy." By the former he means "out of touch, avoiding close relationships, the inability to feel"; by the latter he means "lack of passion, emotion or excitement." He finds some healing for this modern sickness in the therapy methods of his science, which "has led to a resurgence of the primacy of feeling."[5]

In an effort to cope with the artificial restraints of our contemporary culture, some psychologists have introduced encounter groups. Techniques are used to break down the conditioning that stifles a person's awareness of his whole body and makes him inhibited in communicating with others. Providing flesh-to-flesh contact is one means for helping people escape from unhealthy isolation and recover optimum human interaction. Julius Fast demonstrates that positive results can come from tactile encounters. He states: "We cannot achieve emotional freedom in many cases unless we can reach through our personal space, through the masks we set up as protection, to touch and fondle and interact physically with other people." Fast illustrates the effectiveness of personal contact by telling of an experience he had while teaching teen-agers at a church school. On finding it impossible to communicate verbally with one troublemaker, he resorted to tickling the boy until he promised to behave. From then on the boy became a cooperative member of the class.[6]

The great popularity of sensitivity training is an indication that many adults crave affection, which they have lacked since the days of childhood stroking. Psychologist Carl Rogers has called it "the most important social invention of this century."[7] It has been given this theological assessment by James Clark: "Sensitivity training can teach people to see God and Christ in places where they might never have thought possible."[8]

Church associations are at least as out of touch—literally—as other groups in our society. The recently coined and constantly used term "uptight" is an appropriate description of those characteristically distant and stiff gatherings. Holding hands or bodily stroking is unusual when people meet together as Christians, and kissing is rare. They have so internalized the "Don't touch!" parental injunction that they act as if Moses brought down from on high a commandment "Thou shalt not touch!" Most church officers would probably ask for the resignation of a minister who had a habit of kissing members of his congregation, especially if he explained that he was trying to convey the spirit of Jesus. Such officers have been taught by our culture that physical expressions of endearment are exclusively sexual signals and are therefore indecent for any except spouses and the mothers of infants.

THE BIBLICAL CUSTOM

How different this modern behavioral pattern is from the mode of interaction that was characteristic of men and women in the ancient Hebrew and early Christian cultures! As we have seen, the patriarchs, prophets, and apostles demonstrated their feelings with much less reserve than we usually do today. It is especially instructive to examine the role of kissing, one nonverbal way by which they often communicated. Since labial conjunction involves a considerable amount of vulnerability, the extent of its practice in a society serves as a good indicator of that society's general openness toward interpersonal relations.

In Old Testament times kissing most commonly occurred in affectionate exchanges between relatives. For example, Jacob kissed his uncle, Joseph his father, Moses his brother, and David his son (Gen. 29:13; 50:1; Ex. 4:27; II Sam. 14:33). The kiss had several purposes. It was a way of greeting and of expressing farewell. Accordingly, when David and Jonathan met "they kissed one another, and wept with one another" (I Sam. 20:41). Likewise, when Naomi was planning to leave her daughters-in-law, "Orpah kissed her mother-in-law, but Ruth clung to her" (Ruth 1:14).

Kissing was also a way of communicating forgiveness. In the patriarchal saga there is a story of the twin brothers Esau and Jacob, who were alienated because Jacob had stolen Esau's birthright. Yet, after twenty years of separation, this reconciliation took place: "Esau ran to meet him, and embraced him, and fell on his neck and kissed him, and they wept" (Gen. 33:4). Another dramatic confrontation in Genesis conveys a similar renewal of fellowship. Joseph accepted his older brothers, who had sold him into slavery, in this manner: "He kissed all his brothers and wept upon them; and after that his brothers talked with him" (Gen. 45:15). It was Joseph's body language more than his reassuring words that convinced the frightened brothers that they were genuinely forgiven.

Most instances of kissing in Jewish Scriptures are between members of the same sex, but caresses between men and women are also mentioned. Seemingly it was love at first sight for Jacob, for he kissed Rachel when they first met (Gen. 29:11). In the Song of Songs the bride expresses this longing: "O that he would kiss me with the kisses of his mouth" (S. of Songs 1:2). The bridegroom reciprocates with this admission: "Your kisses are like the best wine that goes down smoothly, gliding over lips and teeth" (ch. 7:9). The passion that transpires between that couple can best be compared to the strong love communicated by Auguste Rodin's acclaimed sculpture, *The Kiss*.

Since the kiss is a symbol of affection, the treacherous man used kisses in a perverted manner as a cover for deception. A Hebrew proverb expresses this crisply: "Profuse are the kisses of an enemy" (Prov. 27:6). Jacob provides an instance of this when he kisses Isaac before stealing his blessing (Gen. 27:27; cp. II Sam. 20:9). Warning is given of prostitutes who catch clients by kissing them (Prov. 7:13).

The Hebrew emphasis on the kiss is continued in the New Testament. Jesus endorsed the kiss of hospitality and was warmly appreciative of the woman who kissed his feet fervently.[9] In his unsurpassed story of God's relationship to man, Jesus told of a compassionate father who embraced and kissed his prodigal son in a display of full forgiveness that no words could convey (Luke 15:20). The most famous kiss in the Gospels, and perhaps on historical record, is the kiss of Judas (Mark 14:45). That kiss was especially poignant because the deceit and cowardice it expressed was the opposite of the sincerity and courage of his master.

Jesus' appreciation of the kiss was one way in which he displayed his Jewish conviction that man was a psychosomatic unity. Frequently the Gospels refer to him touching and being touched by males and females. They tell of his technique for healing the sick: "He laid his hands on every one of them." A leper, commonly treated as an untouchable, was healed by means of a touch (Luke 4:40; 5:13). Jesus held that the ideal life involves "becoming like children" (Matt. 18:3). For children, tactility is important: to snuggle, hug, and kiss is at least as prominent a way of communicating as to talk.

In his story of the Grand Inquisitor, Fyodor Dostoevsky shows comprehension of the significance of the kiss in the Gospels. After a sinister minister of the ecclesiastical establishment castigates his prisoner Jesus for championing freedom and love rather than fear and vengeance, the tale concludes in this poignant way:

> When the Inquisitor ceased speaking he waited some time for his Prisoner to answer him. His silence weighed down upon him. He saw that the Prisoner had listened intently all the time, looking gently in his face and evidently not wishing to reply. The old man longed for him to say something, however bitter and terrible. But he suddenly approached the old man in silence and softly kissed him on his bloodless aged lips.[10]

Dostoevsky's fiction is similar to the record of early Christian tradition by Clement of Alexandria. He states that James, the first apostle to be martyred, forgave the repentant man who brought him into court, said "Peace be with you," and kissed him before being beheaded.[11]

Possibly because of docetic bias, New Testament translators misrepresent Jesus as not kissing anyone. Mark 10:21 is a case in point: there Jesus' love is overly internalized in English versions and thereby a characteristic behavioral trait of the ancient Jew is lost. The account of Jesus' response to the rich young ruler is typically translated in this way: "His heart warmed to him" (NEB) However, the same Greek verb used here is sometimes properly rendered "kissed" or "embraced" in other early Christian and non-Christian literature.[12] Translators evidently do not consider it appropriate to picture Jesus as participating in an outward demonstration of affection that might suggest sexual overtones. Yet, textual scholars point out that the verse under consideration might well be translated: "He kissed him."[13] Such a translation correctly suggests that Jesus *acted* as well as *felt* lovingly and, like other rabbis, engaged in expressions of endearment toward those to whom he wanted to extend his love.

The kiss literally effects a union of breaths, and figuratively an interaction of spirits. Both the Hebrew term *ruach* and the Greek term *pneuma* ambivalently refer to wind, breath, and human or divine spirit. Accordingly, a Genesis writer tells of clay becoming a human self after being in-spired by God. In the Fourth Gospel the victorious Jesus brought a new vitality to his apostles when "he breathed on them and said to them, 'Receive the Holy Spirit' " (John 20:22). The picture language here may be that of an embrace similar to Elisha's mouth-to-mouth resuscitation of a child (II Kings 4: 32–35). John Donne relates the old and new creation by this figure: "In the Old Testament, at first God kissed man, and so breathed the breath of life, and made him a man; in the New Testament Christ kissed man, he breathed the breath of everlasting life, the Holy Ghost, into his apostles, and so made the man a blessed man."[14] In a study of the sacred kiss, Nicolas Perella suggests that the kiss had an extraordinary significance in the New Testament because it "could figure as a symbolic vehicle for the immaterial Spirit (Breath) indwelling in the spiritualized bodies of the brethren."[15]

The apostles continued the ancient Jewish positive regard for tactile demonstrations in the "laying on of hands" and in the kiss. Judging from the five exhortations to kiss fellow Christians in the New Testament letters, the exchange was common wherever they met. Peter called it a "kiss of love" (I Peter 5:14)[16] Paul frequently concluded his letters with this request: "Greet one another with a holy kiss." But what was meant by a *holy* kiss? "Holy" is today associated with "godly," which, in turn, connotes something ethereal and nonphysical. Does this mean that Paul did not sanction a tender physical touching? Also "holy" can mean that which is separate from ordinary impurities. Does "holy" kissing thus imply that kissing, as commonly practiced, is defiling? To answer either question in the affirmative would be to misunderstand Paul's use of terminology. The apostle called the kiss "holy" *(hagion)* because it was to be exchanged by the "holy ones" *(hagioi)*. By the term *hagioi* Paul referred to ordinary Christians who were far from undefiled (e.g., Rom. 16:15; I Cor. 16:1; Phil. 1:1). Thus he enjoined all Christians, male and female, to engage in the customary fraternal kiss.

What was the purpose of the Christian kiss? James Moffatt calls it "a natural symbol of the intense family consciousness in Christendom."[17] The early church gathered in homes, and members tended to regard their fellowship as a kind of extended family. Like Jesus, they tended to hold those bound by a common understanding of God's will closer than blood relations (Mark 3:35; Rom. 8:29; 16:13; I Tim. 1:2). Fellow members were thus deserving of at least as intimate an embrace as physical kin. Consequently, leaders of the Ephesian church, most of whom were Gentiles, hugged and kissed him in a manner reminiscent of the affection expressed among members of a Hebrew household (Acts 20:37).

POST-BIBLICAL PRACTICES

In early church history the kiss was a regular part of the liturgy. Justin Martyr described the Eucharist celebration thus: "We greet each other with a kiss. . . . When the president of the brethren has given thanks and the whole congregation has assented, those whom we call deacons give to each of those present a portion of the consecrated bread and wine and water."[18] Writing around A.D. 200, Tertullian indicated that no congregational worship was complete without the kiss. Inasmuch as kissing between the sexes was practiced, that Latin father advised Christian maidens against marrying pagans. He recognized that their husbands might become suspicious on seeing them kissing Christian brothers.[19]

The kiss was also endorsed by some bishops in the late patristic era. Cyprian thought that Christians should act like love doves! He drew this analogy: "The Holy Spirit came as a dove. . . . Doves pass their lives in mutual intercourse, marking their peace and concord with a kiss and fulfilling in every point the law of unanimity. The church should exhibit their innocence and practice their affection."[20] The interpretation given by Cyril of Jerusalem also harmonizes with the Biblical outlook: "This kiss is the sign that our souls are mingled together and that we banish all remembrance of injury." Cyril placed the kiss in the liturgy prior to the offering because Jesus had said: "If you are offering your gift at the altar and there remember that your brother has something against you, . . . first be reconciled with your brother."[21] John Chrysostom instructed Christians to kiss when they congregated so as to simulate the apostolic fellowship in which participants joined together with "one heart." He provided imagery for the conjoining of lips that was unusual: "The Holy Spirit has made us temples of Christ. Therefore when we kiss each other's mouths, we are kissing the entrance of the temple." "The kiss is to be given as a fuel to love, that it may generate affection."[22]

During the patristic era there were other church leaders who were embarrassed by the "kiss of love" because they were fearful that it would lead to erotic excesses. The first to criticize the kiss was Athenagoras in the late second century. That apologist even thought that somewhere in Scripture there was a prohibition against kissing a second time because of finding the act enjoyable. He gravely warned: "The kiss, or rather the salutation, should be given with the greatest care; since, if it is defiled by the slightest evil thought, it excludes us from eternal life."[23] Clement of Alexandria had similar apprehensions about the kissing custom among Christians. He complained:

> There are those who do nothing but make the churches resound with kisses. . . . The shameless use of the kiss, which ought to be mystic, occasions foul suspicions and evil reports among the heathen. . . . Do you not know that spiders, merely by touching the mouth, afflict men with pain? And often kisses inject the poison

of licentiousness. It is then very manifest to us that a kiss is not Christian love."[24]

Church regulations emerged to counteract the pleasurable poten-tialities of the kiss. The fourth-century Apostolic Constitutions stated: "Let the men give the men, and the women give the women, the Lord's kiss."[25] A seventh-century code prescribed forty days of penance for a priest who touched or kissed a woman.[26] These stultify-ing restrictions contributed to the discontinuance of what began as a spontaneous intimate exchange among all Christians. The strictures against kissing fit into Geoffrey May's assessment of the general tendency of early Christianity. He wrote: "Within a period of four centuries Christianity had exchanged its attitude of emotional expres-sion for an attitude of emotional suppression."[27]

Why did the warmth of social intercourse among Christians di-minish during the late patristic period? From the citations given above it is apparent that some churchmen did not understand the original meaning of the kiss and saw it only as an opportunity for erotic fondling. In overreacting to those with a lustful outlook, the church devalued the "kiss of love."

Some strong currents within Roman morality also contributed to the diminution of emotional expression among Christians. Kissing was frowned upon by pagans who wanted to drain off the emotions from life. Some church leaders found the passionless ideal of the Stoics attractive and attempted to blend it into the Christian life-style.[28] The impact of Stoicism on Roman culture may be detected in this report by Plutarch: "Cato ejected a man from the Senate for kissing his own wife in the presence of his daughter." Although Plutarch indicates that Cato's reaction was probably too severe, he states: "It is indecent for people to caress and kiss and embrace each other in the presence of others."[29] A. D. Nock, in an erudite treat-ment of Roman history, has pointed out that the English poet Swin-burne made a causal error in this bitter charge: "Thou hast con-quered, O pale Galilean; the world has grown grey from thy breath." After describing the asceticism of Greco-Roman civilization, Nock offers this corrective: "We know that paganism had of itself gone far in the direction of grayness."[30]

From the medieval period onward, the kiss has been retained only vestigially in the church. In Western Catholicism an impersonal "kiss of peace" has prevailed in which celebrants kiss an object at the altar during high mass rather than touch a person with their lips. Jesuit Josef Jungmann claims that this practice was taken over from the pagan practice of kissing idol statues.[31] In Eastern Orthodoxy celebrants kiss one another at the Easter rites. Certain Anabaptist groups —the Amish, Brethren, and Mennonites—incorporate the kiss in their Communion and foot-washing observances. They also used to exchange the kiss as a nonliturgical greeting, but that is no longer commonly practiced. From over a century ago there comes this record of a Shaker meeting: "Elder Brother said, 'Let us arise from our knees and greet each other with a kiss of charity' . . . so we all went to hugging and kissing in good earnest, and loved a heap."[32]

In some experimental liturgies the Christian significance of the touch has been resurrected, but the expression has usually been a handshake rather than a kiss. This switch may have been prompted by J. B. Phillips' widely circulated New Testament translation-paraphrase, which reads "handshake" instead of "kiss" in Paul's letters. However, in one wedding service the bride and groom, after kissing each other, kissed another member of the wedding party and the chain response continued until all attending had been bussed. But this was so unusual that it was reported in an international news magazine. Also, at an Assembly of the World Council of Churches in Sweden, worship services were held in which the focus was on the sense of touch, including the "kiss of love."[33]

The history of Christianity shows a drift toward minimizing personal encounter. Emotional ardor has been largely displaced by a passionless propriety. The church has become like a museum: "Please do not touch" directives tell us that the curators hope that our experience will be exclusively by means of our remote senses. The theme of much of church history is "carnival" in its Latin meaning: "farewell to flesh." Ironically, in the name of the Incarnate One, modes of enfleshment of the Christian spirit have been banned. Somewhere along the way the unfeeling, Unmoved Mover of Aristotle has tended to take precedence over the Moved Mover of the gospel as the symbol of perfection.

Atypical of most Christians have been those early Mormons who, like the ancient Jews, believed that physical intimacy and genuine religion are bound together inextricably. For example, Orson Hyde, president of the Quorum of Twelve Apostles, believed that Jesus and other Biblical personalities engaged in a full range of heterosexual caressing. Therefore he speculated on how Jesus would have fared in his Victorian era:

> If Jesus Christ were now to pass through the most pious countries in Christendom with a train of women, such as used to follow him, fondling about him, combing his hair, anointing him with precious ointment, washing his feet with tears, and wiping them with the hair of their heads and unmarried, or even married, he would be mobbed, tarred, and feathered, and rode not on an ass, but on a rail.[34]

CONCLUSION

If Christians were to revive the way in which the Biblical figures demonstrated their feelings, we would have a more authentic sense of personal communion. Bodily emotion is inseparable from love, the central theme of the Judeo-Christian religion. Tactile encounters often afford an apt analogy for expressing this highest quality of divine revelation and human aspiration. For example, the experience of love has been described in this way: "It's like crawling out of an old tough calloused skin that has always protected and letting another human being touch me on the new inner skin that's so sensitive and close to my inside."[35]

Since touch is a touchstone of the genuineness of affection, clergymen might well deescalate their bombardment of the head, occasionally descend from the pulpit, exchange their robes for towels, and work on other parts of the anatomy. Unfortunately the clerical model has usually been Peter, whose judgmental messages are reported in Acts. Why not pay more attention to Mary and others noted for giving tender massages? She is the one figure in the Gospels who anticipated Jesus' request that his followers "ought to wash one another's feet" (John 12:1–3; 13:14). Possibly it was from that woman at Bethany that he came to a full awareness of the significance of foot washing.

Harvey Cox has recently puzzled over the way in which Christians have ignored their leader's unequivocal instruction regarding foot washing that is "more explicit than the words Jesus used to institute communion." Cox suggests: "Perhaps the first step toward the reintroduction of our lost sense of touch in Christianity would be to start following Jesus' command and example about foot washing. It would unite people in service, touching and cleansing."[36] Bernard Gunther, on the basis of what has been found effective for expressing affection at Esalen encounter groups, advises washing one another's feet and then massaging them with oil.[37] It is significant that the warmly human Pope John XXIII revived in Rome the Maundy Thursday custom of foot washing in remembrance of Jesus' washing his apostles' feet.

Religion cannot be adequately treated as a surface issue either literally or figuratively. It is more than skin deep, and so it is of little value unless it also penetrates the brain. But just as the sense of touch is a principal avenue for providing data to our brain, so the tactile sense should be a means of stimulating our true self. Those who are untouched by religion may have had an upbringing in which caressing and other skin communication was not adequately employed to signal acceptance, unity, and other psychospiritual meanings.

What type of touch is the most appropriate Christian greeting? The depth of relationship determines the proper physical gesture. A woman would understandably be offended if, on the one hand, her husband greeted her with a handshake or, on the other hand, a stranger greeted her with a kiss. Her negative response would be due to her judgment that the kiss is appropriate for family members but is not warranted for outsiders. If we could restore the early church's view that all Christians belong to one large, joyous household, then the "kiss of love" would be the most suitable way of signifying welcome, reconciliation, inspiration, affection, and farewell. A mouth-to-mouth resuscitation of the familial gesture of apostolic Christianity might keep the church from rubbing people the wrong way as it copes with the social problems of "future shock" society.

8

The Sensuous Semitic Paradise

THE TERM "Paradise" and its cognates in Semitic and European languages comes from the Avestan word *pairdaeza*. In the ancient Persian language it referred to an enclosed park (from *pairi*, "around," and *daeza*, "wall"). Xenophon, the first to transliterate it into Greek, always used *paradeisos* in reference to playgrounds for Persian noblemen. He states: "Cyrus had a palace and a large *paradeisos* full of wild animals which he used to hunt. . . . Through the middle of this park flows the Maeander River."[1] Josephus tells of the "hanging *paradeisoi*" of Babylon that Nebuchadnezzar constructed.[2] To please his queen, who came from a mountainous region, he simulated a forested hill by planting a variety of flora on terraced slopes. In the Hellenistic era, Antipater of Sidon included that magnificent site among the Seven Wonders of the World.

THE HEBREW PARADISE

In some late books of the Hebrew Bible *pairdaeza* is rendered *pardes*, meaning "orchard" or "forest." Solomon is represented as excelling at *pardes* construction in which all kinds of fruit trees were planted (Eccl. 2:5). In another book he is represented as comparing the cheeks of his bride with a *pardes* laden with luscious pomegranates (S. of Songs 4:13). The only other reference to *pardes* is by Nehemiah, who requested the Persian king Artaxerxes to contribute timbers from his royal *pardes* for use in rebuilding the gates of Jerusalem (Neh. 2:8).

The Palestinian writer of the Yahwist creation story most probably had Mesopotamia in mind when he located the ideal garden "in the East." The river that originated in Eden divided and flowed throughout the earth. Precious metals and stones were found in the vicinity of one stream. Primal man was a vegetarian, so not even animals were slaughtered. Beasts and birds were found to be unfit for human sexual companionship, but man found delight in becoming "one flesh" with woman. Although Gerhard von Rad can discover nothing in this story about "sensual enjoyment,"[3] it is manifestly sensuous, with bountiful provision for satisfying human hunger and sexual appetites.

The Septuagint translators utilized the term *paradeisos* not only to refer to any glorious garden; they also used it as a proper noun in reference to a primordial garden planted by Yahweh. It was especially appropriate to use a term borrowed from Mesopotamian culture to refer to a story which originated in that area. The Paradise of Eden is based on myths that were prominent a millennium earlier. The place name given that ideal environment is the same as the Sumerian term *eden*, meaning plain or steppe. "Dilmun" is the special Sumerian designation for a divine paradise which was located in "the place where the sun rises." In the "Enki and Ninhursag" epic, the waters of the earth issued forth from Dilmun and they caused fruitful plants to abound. It was an idyllic place where sickness, death, and violence were not troublesome. There "the lion kills not, the wolf snatches not the lamb . . . , the sick-headed says not 'I am sick-headed,' its old woman says not 'I am an old woman,' its old man says not 'I am an old man.' " Zuisudra, the Sumerian counterpart of the Biblical Noah, was translated to Dilmun because he received divine favor.[4] In the parallel Babylonian epic, flood survivors Utnapishtim and his wife were made immortal by the gods and were taken to a distant place to reside "at the mouth of the rivers."[5] In that same epic, Gilgamesh found a marvelous garden containing gems and lush fruit.[6]

The divine *paradeisos* motif appears at several other places in the Greek Bible. In the patriarchal saga the well-watered Jordan valley is compared with the *"paradeisos* of the Lord"* (Gen. 13:10). The Promised Land is often represented as a paradisal land, "flowing with milk and honey" (e.g., Ex. 3:8; Josh. 5:6). It is described in Balaam's oracle thus:

How fair are your tents, O Jacob; your dwelling-places, O Israel!
Like long rows of palms, like *paradeisoi* by a river,
Like aloes planted by the Lord, like cedars beside the water!
(Num. 24:5–6)

In one of the last sermons attributed to Moses, this motif continues: "The Lord your God is bringing you to a fine land, a land of streams, of springs and underground waters gushing out in hill and valley, a land of wheat and barley, of vines, fig-trees, and pomegranates, a land of olives, oil, and honey. It is a land where you can eat and never famish, where you will not lack anything" (Deut. 8:7-9).

The prophets frequently alluded to a grand restoration of nature. Indeed, Walther Eichrodt claims that the return of Paradise is at the heart of the futurist visions of the prophets.[7] Amos, for example, declared that "mountains shall drip sweet wine" (Amos 9:13). Isaiah of Jerusalem predicted that there will be pristine peacefulness among all creatures. The harmony that will reign between nature and nature's God is exquisitely pictured:

> The wolf shall dwell with the lamb,
>
> .   .   .   .   .   .
>
>   and a little child shall lead them.
>
> .   .   .   .   .   .
>
> For the earth shall be full of the knowledge of the Lord
>   as the waters cover the sea.
> (Isa. 11:6–9)

Some postexilic prophets also announced that nature will regain its original fecundity. "The Lord will comfort Zion," Isaiah promised,

> Turning the wilderness into an Eden,
> Her thirsty plains into a *paradeisos* of the Lord.
> (Isa. 51:3)

Ezekiel repeatedly spoke of "Eden, the *paradeisos* of God" (Ezek. 28:13; 31:8–9). In accord with the Genesis Paradise, it contains precious stones and a life-giving river. The trees on the banks will bear fresh fruit monthly and their leaves will be used for medication (Ezek. 47:1–12).

Some Jewish books of the intertestamental period continue the prophetic theme of a Paradise that will appear in the last days and that will be the same as the first. Enoch visited a terrestrial Paradise, a place full of fragrant trees, where God's elect will dwell (I Enoch 20:7; 32:3; 60:8). Another apocalypse states that the priest-Messiah "will open the gates of Paradise, take away the sword which threatened Adam, and give the saints to eat of the tree of life" (Testament of Levi 18:10–11). "The saints shall rest in Eden, and in the new Jerusalem shall the righteous rejoice" (Testament of Dan 5:12). A celestial Paradise replaces one on earth in some of the later apocalypses (II Enoch 8:1–2; Apocalypse of Moses 40:2; IV Ezra 4:8).

PARADISE IN EARLY CHRISTIANITY

Paradeisos occurs three times in the New Testament, but no explanation is given by any of the three writers who use the term. This suggests that *paradeisos* had a commonly accepted meaning in the milieu of the apostolic church as a result of the widespread Jewish speculation on the concept: The Aramaic term *pardesa* probably lies behind Luke's record of Jesus' words to the penitent thief, "Today you shall be with me in *paradeisos*" (Luke 23:43). In his teachings Jesus pictured Paradise as a banquet, with Abraham as the master of ceremonies (Luke 16:23). It would be prepared for those who had been faithful to God before their physical death (Luke 22:28–30). Such a splendid supper was also conceived of in ancient Judaism. A midrash states: "In the hereafter the Holy One, blessed be he, will prepare a banquet for the righteous in the Garden of Eden and there will be no need to provide balsam or perfumes, because a northern and southern breeze will blow through all the aromatic plants so that they yield their fragrance."[8]

If Jesus thought of Paradise as a place, it is difficult to ascertain whether it was for him a compartment of the subterranean Hades (or Sheol), a renovated area on earth, or a heavenly abode. The "apostolic father" Papias may have thought that Jesus spoke of the future in terrestrial terms. Irenaeus claimed that the apostle John transmitted to Papias this saying of Jesus: "The days shall come when vines will grow, every one of which will have ten thousand branches . . . and every grape when pressed will yield twenty-five barrels of wine."[9] Some Jewish apocalypses that date back to, or before, the beginning of the Christian era express that fantasy of abundance in virtually the same way (II Baruch 29:5; I Enoch 10:19).

When John the Baptist displayed misgivings over Jesus' fulfillment of prophetic expectations, Jesus related his healing ministry to the paradisal imagery of Isaiah (Luke 7:22). In a passage to which Jesus alluded, Isaiah declared that "the desert shall rejoice and burst into flower," "the eyes of the blind shall be opened," "the ears of the deaf shall be unstopped," "the lame shall leap up like a deer," and "waters shall spring up in the wilderness" (Isa. 35:1, 5–6). The Gospel writers viewed Jesus' ministry as a foretaste of Paradise. As "the water which quenches all thirst," "the bread of life," "the resurrection and the life," and "the fruit of the vine," he personified much of its glory (John 4:14; 6:35; 11:25; Mark 14:25). The state of resurrection, which Jesus inaugurated, is symbolized in the Gospel of John by wine flowing at a wedding party (John 2:1–11), the elimination of corrupted forms of worship (John 2:12–22), the restoration of lost health (John 4:46 to 5:15; 9:1–34), the abundant provision for human needs (John 6:1–13), the safety of a fold guarded by a good shepherd (John 10:1–18), and the permanent friendship that results from intimate union (John 15:1–17; 20:1 to 21:23). Paradise is here partly detemporalized or demythologized and is regarded as an immediate experience of Christians. In the Johannine writings "eternal life" is treated more as a quality of being realizable now than as an infinite quantity of time at some place in the cosmos.[10] The focus is on adding life to one's years rather than on adding years to one's life.

Paul referred to "the third heaven" into which he was "caught up" as *paradeisos*. He saw and heard some things in that ecstatic experience that he could not communicate by speech (II Cor. 12:2–3). The apocryphal Apocalypse of Paul may be right in assuming that Paul's conception of "the third heaven" was similar to that recorded in II Enoch, a Jewish apocalypse composed during the apostolic era.[11] Paul, who was beset with considerable suffering when he mentioned his revelation of Paradise, would no doubt have found comforting the story of Enoch's rapture. Enoch's assumption to the place of highest bliss is described in this way:

Two men . . . carried me up on to the third heaven and set me down in the midst of Paradise, and a place unknown in goodness of appearance. Every tree sweet-flowering, every fruit ripe, all man-

ner of food perpetually bubbling with all pleasant smells, and four
rivers flowing by. . . , and the tree of life is at that place, at which
God rests when he goes up into Paradise, and that tree is ineffable
for the goodness of its sweet scent, and another olive tree alongside
was always discharging the oil of its fruit. And there is no tree there
without fruit, and every tree is blessed. And the angels guarding
the Paradise are very bright and serve the Lord all days with
incessant voice and sweet singing. And I said: "How very sweet is
this place!" And the two men answered me: "This place, Enoch,
is prepared for the righteous, who suffer offence in their lives and
spite in their souls, and avert their eyes from injustice and make
righteous judgment, to give bread to the hungering, to clothe the
naked and cover them with a garment, to raise the fallen, and help
the wronged, who walk before God's face and serve him alone; now
for these is this place prepared for an eternal inheritance. (II
Enoch 8–9)

The first and last books of the Christian Bible complement each
other in that the Paradise motif is central to both. John of Patmos
is directed to write thus to the Ephesian church, in the name of the
resurrected Jesus: "To him who conquers I will grant to eat of the
tree of life, which is in the *paradeisos* of God" (Rev. 2:7). The last
two chapters of Revelation enlarge on this eschatological symbol.
There will be a renewal of all creation which, like the uncorrupted
original Paradise, will be a place for close fellowship between God and
his people. Moreover, it will provide opportunities for intimate relations between men and women and for appreciation of abundant and
beautiful nature. It is pictured as a "new Jerusalem, coming down out
of heaven from God, prepared as a bride adorned for her husband."
This gives an earthly setting for the perfect society and employs
wedding imagery to describe its grandeur. John here carries forward
the bridal figure that he introduced earlier. There are sensuous references to the bride's lovely dress, to the marriage supper, and to the
bride's invitation to her husband to "come" (Rev. 19:7–9; 22:17). A
similar symbol is given by a midrash in which God welcomes the
blessed dead in the same way that Solomon in the Song of Songs woos
his adoring spouse—with the words, "I have come into my garden,
my dear bride."[12]

As did the first Paradise, the final Paradise will abound in precious metals and stones. The pearly gates, jasper walls, and golden streets suggest everlastingness as well as dazzling beauty. Neither moth nor rust consumes those materials. The river and the vegetation are also wonderful. "On either side of the river stood a tree of life, which yields twelve crops of fruit, one for each month of the year; the leaves of the trees serve for the healing of the nations." God's people partake of the fruit and drink "the water of life."

During the patristic era, the Biblical imagery of a lush Paradise was utilized by some church spokesmen. In the fourth century, Lactantius rhapsodized: "The rocky mountains shall drip with honey; streams of wine shall run down, and rivers flow with milk. . . . Beasts shall not be nourished by blood, nor birds by prey; but all things shall be peaceful and tranquil."[13] Similar sentiments were expressed during that same century by Syrian Christians. Aphraates wrote: "The air is pleasant and tranquil; a bright light shines; the trees bear fruit constantly, and their leaves never fall. They emit a sweet fragrance, and in their shade the souls of the departed eat and are never glutted."[14] The ascetic Ephraim thought of Paradise as the reversal of his present state:

> I saw the swelling places of the just, and they themselves, dripping with ointments, giving forth pleasant odors, wreathed in flowers and decked with fruits. . . . Whoever has abstained from wine on earth, for him do the vines of Paradise yearn. . . . And if a man has lived in chastity, the women receive him in a pure bosom, because he was a monk and did not fall into the bosom and bed of earthly love.[15]

THE MOSLEM PARADISE

Some authorities on Mohammed claim that it was from Syrian Christianity that the prophet derived his conception of Paradise.[16] However, unlike the Syrian monks, he thought of the afterlife as a continuation of what gave him satisfaction during his life in Arabia. He lived for some years with his wives in Medina, a verdant oasis that produced delicious fruit.

Mohammed was faithful to his Semitic tradition in affirming the positive value of material creation. He inquired: "Who dares to forbid man the enjoyment of his things of beauty, of the delicacies of food, or raiment and other good things of God's bounty?"[17] Also included by him among these "things of beauty" are human bodies, domestic animals, perfumes, and other delectable features of the natural world.[18]

It was Mohammed's conviction that praise to Allah should be combined with holistic enjoyment in the present life and in the more ideal life to come. Bodily and spiritual joys are combined in the picture of Paradise *(Firdaus)* given in the Koran. Facets of that realm can be seen in the following excerpts:

> Enter Paradise, you and your wives, and be glad![19]
> The people of Paradise are happily engaged, both men and their wives are in the shade, reclining on bridal couches.[20]
> Therein are streams of unpolluted water, sweet milk, tasty wine, and clear honey.[21]
> Gardens of Eden! They enter them wearing gold and pearl bracelets and silk garments. And they say: "Praise be to Allah who has taken away our sorrow. Truly, our Lord is forgiving, bountiful, who by his grace has placed us in the mansion of eternity where toil does not touch us nor can weariness affect us."[22]
> There is, for the devout, a blissful place—enclosed gardens and vineyards, and houris with swelling breasts, their peers in age, and a brimming cup.[23]
> In gardens of delight, . . . reclining face to face on decorated couches, eternal youths wait on them with goblets and ewers and a cup from a pure spring. No headaches shall they feel therefrom, nor shall their wits be dimmed! There are such fruits as they shall choose, and such flesh of fowl as they desire. And theirs shall be the houris, with large dark eyes as lovely as pearls, a reward for what they have done. They hear there no vain talk nor recrimination, only the saying, "Peace, Peace!" . . . The houris have been created anew as virgins.[24]
> Upon that day faces will be resplendent, looking toward their Lord.[25]

Who are those sensual houris who provide companionship? The Koran frequently refers to them as wives of the faithful.[26] Also, reference is made to *purified* spouses in Paradise.[27] In the earliest Islamic tradition, Mohammed explains: "The houris are devout wives, and those who with grey hair and watery eyes died in old age. After death Allah remakes them into virgins."[28] Those men and women who have been chosen for Paradise have been transformed by their resurrection; consequently rejuvenated bodies have replaced the decrepit physical state in which they may have left their earthly existence.

Some Moslems have expressed skepticism toward the concept of the afterlife in their orthodox tradition and have preferred to emphasize a this-worldly Paradise. The twelfth-century Persian poet Omar Khayyám was intrigued by Mohammed's promise of houris, but opted posthaste for present companionship for fear that posthumous relations with lovely maidens might never transpire.[29] Edward Fitz-Gerald's *Rubáiyát* eloquently paraphrases Omar's witty musings:

> A Book of Verses underneath the Bough,
> A Jug of Wine, a Loaf of Bread—and Thou
> Beside me singing in the Wilderness—
> Oh, Wilderness were Paradise enow!

> Some for the Glories of This World; and some
> Sigh for the Prophet's Paradise to come;
> Ah, take the Cash, and let the Credit go,
> Nor heed the rumble of a distant Drum![30]

PARADISE IN WESTERN CHRISTIANITY

Ironically, the pagan philosopher Plato has contributed more to the formulation of Christian thought than any church father. He was contemptuous of the paradisal fantasies of Hesiod and the other Greek poets.[31] Plato mocked those who "have the saints lying on couches at a feast, crowned with wreaths, continually drinking wine."[32] Accordingly, Origen and other Christian Platonists criticized those who use sensuous imagery in treating the afterlife. For Origen the teacher, Paradise is an academy where disembodied souls study astronomy.[33]

Augustine assured the faithful that "sensible experience shall be

quite forgotten" in Paradise, for they will be absorbed in contemplat-
ing God.[34] He appropriated Garden of Eden language in reference
to this beatific vision, but only after desensitizing it. Augustine allegorized as follows: "The four rivers of Paradise are the four Gospels; the
fruit trees the saints, and the fruit their works."[35] That ascetic monk,
along with the host of Augustinian Christians over the past fifteen
hundred years, prepared for a presumed nonsensuous realm by attempting to wean themselves away from worldly pleasures. "If we
wish to return to our Father's home," Augustine counseled, "this
world must be used, not enjoyed."[36] A passage from his *Confessions*
shows that love of God is not to be approached by loving his creations:

> What do I love when I love Thee? Not beauty of bodies, nor the
> fair harmony of time, nor the brightness of the light, so gladsome
> to our eyes, nor sweet melodies of varied songs, nor the fragrant
> smell of flowers and ointments and spices, not manna and honey,
> not limbs acceptable to embracements of flesh.[37]

Largely because of the colossal influence of Augustine, sexual love,
delectable food, and pleasant aroma were generally absent from the
Paradise of medieval Europe.[38]

Some Latin Christians conceived of otherworldly joy as consisting
of more than the ceaseless worship of God by singing praises. Tertullian, believing that vengeance is sweet, stated:

> What a city, the new Jerusalem! . . . What sight shall wake my
> wonder? Why my laughter, my joy and exultation? I see all those
> kings, those great kings . . . groaning in the depths of darkness. And
> the magistrates who persecuted the name of Jesus liquifying in
> fiercer flames than they kindled in their rage against Christians![39]

Thomas Aquinas rejected much of the Biblical Paradise in declaring
that there will be no pleasures of food or sex in the future life, nor
will any plants or animals be present. However, the lunar bleakness
will not disturb the inhabitants of heaven, for they will divert themselves by gazing down at the torture of those in hell. As he put it:
"In order that the happiness of the saints may be more delightful to
them and that they may render more copious thanks to God for it,
they are allowed to see perfectly the sufferings of the damned."[40]

A revival of Biblical paradisal imagery was effected in the Reformation era. A sixteenth-century hymn entitled "Jerusalem, My Happy Home" was popular among Protestants until the present century.[41] Two representative stanzas follow:

> Thy gardens and thy gallant walkes
>   Continually are greene
> There groes such sweete and pleasant flowers
>   As noe where eles are seene
>
> .   .   .   .   .   .
>
> There cinomon there sugar groes
>   There narde and balme abound
> What tounge can tell or hart conceiue
>   The ioyes that there are found[42]

The seventeenth-century treatment of Paradise by John Milton has also helped to stimulate Protestant imagination. He described "delicious Paradise" which contains "Trees of noblest kind for sight, smell, taste." Under them Adam and Eve embraced and dined:

> Half her swelling Breast
> Naked met his under the flowing Gold
> of her loose tresses hid.
>
> .   .   .   .   .   .
>
>   Thus these two
> Imparadis't in one anothers arms
> The happier *Eden*, shall enjoy thir fill.
>
> .   .   .   .   .   .
>
> For dinner savourie fruits
>
> .   .   .   .   .
>
>   and thir flowing cups
> With pleasant liquors crown'd.

The Puritan bard hailed the connubial love of that representative couple as "the Crown of all our bliss."[43]

Milton assumed that the world which the Last Adam, Jesus, saved would be no less delightful than the one which Adam lost. In the concluding part of *Paradise Regained*, the victorious Jesus participates in a succulent banquet. The angels

>   set him down
> On a green bank, and set before him spread

> A table of Celestial Food, Divine,
> Ambrosial, Fruits fetcht from the tree of life.
>
> .   .   .   .
>
> A fairer Paradise is founded now
> For *Adam* and his chosen Sons, whom thou
> A Saviour art come down to re-install.[44]

This Puritan vision of Paradise is like the Moslem vision. Both Milton and Mohammed adapted the ancient Semitic imagery, which wondrously blends together the spiritual and sensuous aspects of reality. Neither discerned any significance in the Greek concept of a passionless, disembodied soul.

THE EXISTENTIAL MEANING

Eschatological symbols should not be treated as actual descriptions of the hereafter. Throughout history many Jews, Christians, and Moslems have interpreted mythopoetic language literally and have relied on it as a means for escaping from social responsibilities in the here and now. Criticisms of such childish usage of fantasies abound, especially in our scientific culture. Well known is a parody of a camp meeting song:

> You will eat bye and bye
> In that glorious land above the sky;
> Work and pray, live on hay,
> You'll get pie in the sky when you die.

However, paradisal imagery can be used as a means for self-understanding and for participating more fully in current life. Attempting to conceive of an ideal life *after* death—living lovingly with persons and joyfully with the beauties of nature—can add "life that is life indeed" (I Tim. 6:19) *before* death. Paul Tillich points out that a symbol, whether artistic, political, or religious, "gives us not only a new vision of the human scene, but it opens up hidden depths of our own being."[45] Mircea Eliade likewise states: "The function of the paradisal land of perfect freedom remains unchanged. . . . Archetypes still continue to give meaning to life and to create 'cultural values.' "[46] Even in the above parody, the integration of worship, work,

and sensuous enjoyment by all of God's people has existential significance. Conceiving of a posthumous existence as one of eating goodies
is at least more wholesome than the sadism of those medieval theologians who thought the blessed would give vent to their impulses for
revenge.

On this point some Moslem theologians are better guides to Biblical religion than the dominant Latin theologians. While recognizing
that paradisal descriptions are to be interpreted figuratively and that
the afterlife defies full comprehension,[47] they do not presume to
claim that it will be counter to sensual pleasures of this life. Rather,
utopian language is used to suggest that the resurrected life is continuous with those mind-body qualities that now bring the individual
self to fulfillment. In this regard William M. Watt writes:

> The Islamic world is characterized by its frank acceptance of
> sexuality and its belief that the exercise of sexuality should be a
> normal part of the life of every human being. . . . The Islamic
> acceptance of sexuality is perhaps most noticeable in some of the
> conceptions of Paradise. Some form of sexual delight is included
> in eternal bliss, and there is nothing of the Greek conception
> which makes Paradise a place where man has escaped from his
> body and is thankful for the escape.[48]

Those religions with Semitic roots affirm that Paradise is not less
than the happiest conceivable communal existence in this life. Thus
the ancient spokesmen of those religions utilized symbols that focus
on pleasures derived from the five senses. Assuming that life with
God here and hereafter involves the whole personality, they did not
accept the Orphic doctrine of an immortal soul-substance to be
released from its bodily incarceration. To adapt a metaphor of Paul,
they viewed the body as a sacred shrine, not as a profane prison.
Hence, the proper function of Semitic paradisal language is to sketch
out imaginatively the consummation of a society in which the sacred
and the secular are dovetailed. This speculation can enhance and
illuminate common life if taken as saying something serious—but not
literal—about the goals of human existence.

Life after death, like the nature of God, transcends all human
conceptualizing. Paul advised against taking as factually descriptive

the crude figures that we employ to depict life that transcends time and space. Borrowing the words of Isaiah, the apostle wrote: "Things beyond our seeing, hearing, and imagining have been prepared by God for those who love him" (I Cor. 2:9; Cf. Isa. 64:4). Another New Testament letter also wisely states: "What we shall be has not yet been disclosed" (I John 3:2).

Conclusion

THIS STUDY has presented a variety of ways in which the holistic Biblical view of the person was fleshed out. Dance, an especially apt illustration of the ancient Judeo-Christian life-style, has been seen to be an intricate blending together of the senses, the emotions, and the mind. Havelock Ellis singles out dance as the only art "of which we ourselves are the stuff," and he rightly regards it as "the supreme symbol of the spiritual life."[1] To borrow Snoopy's motto: "To live is to dance; to dance is to live." That comic strip character, according to Robert Short, carries out Jesus' advice to "leap for joy" (Luke 6:23).[2] The creative dancer has been treated as an incarnation of divine law and grace; he expresses techniques acquired through strenuous discipline, yet he extemporizes with a fluidity that transcends the dance manual.

Dance has appropriately been used to symbolize the future paradisal life as well as the present Christian life. Fra Angelico portrayed Magdalene adoring a dancing Jesus on Easter morning. Contemporary theologians Hugo Rahner[3] and Jürgen Moltmann regard the dance as the most eloquent way of describing the resurrected life. Moltmann points out that Christianity has usually thought of the end of history as "an ever-varying round dance of the redeemed in the trinitarian fullness of God, and as the complete harmony of soul and body. It has not hoped for an unearthly heaven of bodyless souls but for a new body penetrated by the spirit and redeemed from the bondage of law and death."[4]

Agapē has been seen to be the tune for the earthly and the heavenly dance. Unlike the uncooperative children whom Jesus observed in the marketplace, the childlike participants of this dance have learned the happiness of mutual reciprocation and of moving in rhythm. They weave in and out of an inclusive fellowship composed of persons of different nations, races, classes, and sexes. Their occasional squabblings do not result in bitterness but are springboards to a fuller reconciliation that is sealed by lilting laughter and sensuous communion.

Each chapter not only has shown the appreciation of bodily sensation in Biblical religion but also has displayed the way in which the church for most of its history has been desensitized through the impact of an alien ascetic philosophy. Plato and his many followers have been the main proponents of a mind-body dualism that has been the most influential psychological viewpoint in Western culture. Through Socrates he argues in the *Phaedo:*

> Surely the *psychē* can best reflect when it is free of all distractions such as hearing or sight or pain or pleasure of any kind—that is, when it ignores the *sōma* and becomes as far as possible independent, avoiding all physical contacts and associations as much as it can, in its search for reality. . . . In despising the *sōma* and avoiding it—and endeavoring to become independent—the philosopher's *psychē* is ahead of all the rest. . . . We make the nearest approach to knowledge if we have the least possible intercourse or communion with the *sōma,* and if we are not infected with its nature, but keep ourselves pure from it, until God shall release us.[5]

Socrates had no use for the *philosōma* (body-lover), for such a person does not, by sublimation, climb the rungs of the metaphysical ladder and escape from the oppressive material realm to the realm completely independent of the senses.[6] He believed that the ideal person was the one who was devoted to pommeling the *sōma* in order to enlarge the dominance of the *psychē.* Thus he drank the hemlock with composure, assuring his friends that the act would speed the removal of his immortal *psychē* from his vile *sōma.* How different was Jesus' bloody Gethsemane struggle and his cry of dereliction from the cross! Oscar Cullmann, in discussing the contrast between these two most influential teachers, points out that Jesus was "thoroughly entangled in the world of the senses."[7]

The radical separation of the spiritual and physical qualities has been a tendency of many of the intellectual and religious leaders who have followed Plato. Seneca, who acknowledged heavy indebtedness to Plato, believed that his spirit was as separable from his flesh as a pilot from a ship.[8] Before committing suicide, he wrote: "Contempt for one's body is a sure sign of freedom."[9] Both of the other outstanding Stoics, Epictetus and Marcus Aurelius, urged abstinence from sensual pleasures.[10] Leading Neoplatonist Plotinus had a dualism of the most extreme sort: "A soul becomes filthy by sinking itself into the alien, by a fall, a descent into body, into matter. . . . In a word, life in the body is itself an evil, but the soul enters its good through virtue, not living the life of couplement, but holding itself apart, even here."[11]

Basil, the fourth-century bishop and father of Greek monasticism, was thoroughly Platonic in his doctrine of man. The following excerpt from his writing even contains Plato's charioteer figure:

> We should supply our souls with all things that are best, through philosophy freeing them, as from a prison, from association with the passions of the body. . . . Purification of the soul . . . consists in scorning the pleasures that arise through the senses. . . . The body in every part should be despised by everyone who does not care to be buried in its pleasures, as it were in slime. . . . We must . . . chastise the body and hold it in check, as we do the violent chargings of a wild horse by smiting it with the whip of reason.[12]

Christian ethics from Basil's time onward has held a tight rein on bodily pleasures. Josef Goldbrunner sees the medieval moral tradition as "a bridle to curb an exuberant *joie de vivre.*" He writes:

> From the first violent eruption of the monastic movement, through the Middle Ages to our own time, the tension between body and spirit remains a constant theme. Spiritualization is the aim of all religious striving. War is declared on the body. The dualism is present in all degrees from open hostility to latent suspicion. . . . Attack is the best form of defense and so the instinctive lower life of the body was resisted with flagellations, fastings, and night watches.[13]

The Catholic philosopher Descartes was the most influential of those who carried the mind-body bifurcation into modern European history. He pictured man as essentially a gargantuan head containing a brilliant mind that nearly eclipses the muscular engine appendage below the neck. He stated his position clearly: "I am nothing other than a thing which thinks, that is to say, a mind or a soul, an understanding or a reason. . . . I am not a collection of members which we call the human body."[14] Elsewhere he affirmed that "the body is nothing other than a statue or machine made of earth, which God forms expressly."[15] Gilbert Ryle has referred to this Platonic-Cartesian opposition between intangible mind and extended matter as "the myth of the ghost in the machine."[16]

By no means has it been only the intelligentsia who have believed that mind and body are fundamentally different kinds of substances. LeRoy Moore argues that the basic moral thrust of Protestant pietism, which has been dominant in American history, has largely consisted of "denying the pleasures of the body for the good of the soul." From the Great Awakening to Billy Graham, Moore cogently contends, there has been this implicit theme: "We humans are not our bodies; we only inhabit or use our bodies."[17]

Friedrich Nietzsche discerningly referred to what was called Christian morality in his Victorian era as "Platonism for the people."[18] He found the Christian frantically devoted to an ethic of excision—a swearing off of particular sensual enjoyments. "To become *perfect*, he was advised to draw in his senses, turtle fashion, to cease all intercourse with earthly things, to shed his mortal shroud: then his essence would remain, the 'pure spirit.' "[19] Elsewhere Nietzsche quipped: "The Christian has no nervous system—he has a contempt for, and a deliberate desire to disregard, the demands of the body."[20]

In our own day Sam Keen also notes the way in which dualism has permeated modern culture:

> Our language, like a practiced magician, tricks us into believing in the existence of two separate entities called mind and body. Mind-body language reflects a persistent schizophrenic experience of the self, a dualism present in most civilized cultures. In Greek experience it was reflected in the dichotomy between soul and body, in

Christianity in the warfare between spirit and flesh, in Victorian society in the tension between reason and emotion. We currently find it in the professional separation of physical and psychological medicine. . . . If we were fully integrated persons we might refer to ourselves as *being* bodyminds rather than as *having* bodies.[21]

Beginning with Platonism and continuing with Freudianism it has been assumed that sense repression is the mother of ingenuity. Human innards are thought to function like a hydraulic system: in order to pump sufficient libidinous energy to keep the gray matter in the top of the head swirling maximally, all systems below must operate at mere survival level. In the belief that mental and spiritual flowering results from pruning the appetites severely, the senses of taste, smell, and touch are allowed to atrophy.

This sublimation theory is based on a highly questionable theory of the self. It is not at all apparent that artistic creativity is stimulated by sensuous abstinence. Indeed, it would be easier to show that the opposite is more characteristic. In any case, Jesus did not abstain from meat, wine, perfumes, and social relations with the opposite sex in order to pursue his vocation without distraction. It is a pity that the monks who shaped orthodoxy have followed the advice of Socrates as portrayed in the *Phaedo* rather than that of Jesus as portrayed in the Gospels.

The pagan glorification of the intangible mind at the expense of bodily desires still disembowels basic Christological doctrine. Some influential contemporary theologians naïvely assume that modern Christians have little difficulty acknowledging that Jesus was fully human. W. D. Davies, for example, has proclaimed that "docetism is dead as a doornail."[22] However, that death notice regarding the most ancient of Christian heresies, which held that Jesus only *appeared* to be human, is premature. A recent comprehensive study of a large American denomination reveals that, of its members, "a minority . . . fully acknowledge the humanity of Jesus." Most Lutherans do not believe that Jesus struggled to discover who he really was or that he had sexual desire.[23] This and other polls show that most Christians believe that Jesus was not subject to nature and that he could even walk on water.[24] In this respect they share the outlook of the docetists, who believed that their phantom Jesus was unaffected by gravitation and thus did not leave an imprint where he "walked." Throughout church history docetists have avoided associating their Savior with a full-orbed emotional life. In response to this viewpoint, New Testament critic John Knox has said:

> If he [Jesus] did not share, at the very deepest levels of his conscious and subconscious life, in our human anxieties, perplexities, and loneliness; if his joys were not characteristic human joys and his hopes, human hopes; if his knowledge of God was not in every part and under every aspect the kind of knowledge which it is given to man, the creature, to have—then he was not a true human being, he was not made man, and the Docetists were essentially right. [25]

This docetic tendency has not been arrested by the form and redaction critics that are now at center stage in New Testament criticism. While their approach is often quite helpful for understanding Christian origins, some of them believe that even the Synoptic Gospels afford little insight into the historical person who founded Christianity. The nebulous figure that emerges from many of their studies is frequently more of a discarnate spirit than a flesh-and-blood person who was acculturated in Palestinian Judaism. What is called exegesis sometimes results in exit Jesus!

Until the psychosomatic integration of Jesus' personality is recognized, there is little hope for the recovery of holism by those who worship him and who think they should pattern their lives after his. If many twentieth-century Christians disbelieve in Jesus' full humanity, including his sensual and emotional experiences, then it follows that these same Christians will probably be unable to deal wholesomely with their own human nature. They will either actively deny their bodily needs, or not fully integrate their beliefs with their real lives. The former way leads to unproductive suffering; the latter to debilitating guilt feelings. Over against these alternatives, as this book has tried to show, a Bible-based Christology can lead us into a healthy trust of the sensuous and an integrated acceptance of the emotional.

Sam Keen argues convincingly for a "resurrection of the bodily" within the Christian community.

Incarnation, if it is anything more than a "once-upon-a-time" story, means grace is carnal, healing comes through the flesh. . . . The sacred must be rediscovered in what moves and touches us, in what makes us tremble, in what is proximate rather than remote. . . . The church must become involved in the exploration of ways to reawaken a reverence for the body and its rhythms. . . . If the church fails to develop a visceral theology and fails to help modern man rediscover and reverence his flesh and his feelings, it will neglect a source of common grace as well as the seed from which compassion grows.[26]

How can the Christian community implement the viewpoint set forth in this book? Lasting renewal will come when pastors and leaders are able fully to realize the original Judeo-Christian sensitivity, and to feel in their bones the true Biblical integration of the emotions and the mind. Sweeping away their own remaining reservations about the potential goodness of the sensual, they can, through counseling and other methods of pastoral care, guide the development of full-orbed relationships among their parishioners.

In addition to working with individuals, many churches are finding group activities meaningful for achieving holistic goals. The church must learn from the encounter group movement that the senses need to be appreciated and educated as a means of improving self-understanding and interpersonal relationships. The church has a potential that encounter groups usually lack, in that its community is relatively permanent. It is not constricted by having a limit placed on the number of sessions. In encounter groups the explorations of new ways to achieve bodily acceptance may be made too rapidly to be assimilated, and consequently they may be counterproductive. But a church equipped with *steadfast* love as its fundamental motivation can train its members throughout life in sensitivity. Such *agapē* will provide the decades of patience that may be needed to counteract the "thingifying" conditioning of our impersonal and mechanistic culture.

Throughout the Song of Songs there is the refrain, "I beg you . . . that you do not excite passion before it is ready to stir" (S. of Songs 2:7; 3:5; 8:4). Instant intimacy is rejected because *agapē* cannot be artificially contrived. It is unrealistic for church leaders to expect a quick thaw of God's "frozen people"; frostbite therapy needs to be gradual. It might start with a ritual of friendship in the sanctuary, when handshaking with those in adjacent pews is encouraged. Family night suppers might be concluded with holding hands in a circle and with "the kiss of love."

Those supper meetings also provide excellent opportunities for sharing other sensual experiences. What church member does not enjoy the delightful nasal and palatal sensations of the covered-dish meal, where each family has contributed its own tantalizing specialty? Lest it be thought immoral to advocate the enjoyment of food amid global starvation, it should be recognized that the aesthetic pleasure of the intimate senses is not dependent on the quantity or the expense of what is consumed. In the hands of a culinary artist, that which is modestly priced has at least as much potential for healthy and aesthetic pleasure as, for example, the premium cuts of grain-fed beef. The Christian aesthete, unlike the glutton, drinks the cup of pleasure by sips rather than by gulps. Moreover, the religious person, applying an ethic that is universal in world religions, generously gives material things to others because he has found sensate goods have contributed to his abundant life.

Classes in the dances of various ethnic groups could be conducted, affording a means of combining world understanding with physical exercise. Some might "get a kick" spiritually as they develop muscular coordination and body tone in group dances such as the Israeli hora and the Afro-American rumba, or in individually oriented movements such as Chinese t'ai chi (my favorite) and Polynesian hula.

Recommended also are informal discussions of bodily functions and a cultivation of the senses by groups composed of both younger and older generations. To some extent this can be structured within the church school and fellowship programs. However, the setting for optimum interactions may be in home meetings in which several families can establish the trust and intimacy needed for honest sharing.

Love education that is psychosomatic in focus is a much needed supplement to the sex education of public schools, which tends to be heavily physiological. The isolation of spiritual from fleshly concerns has always been the cause of sexual irresponsibility. As one who regularly teaches a college course in religion and sexuality, I am continually aware of the gap between technological know-how and philosophical know-why. American youth are doubtless the best trained in history in the "facts of life," but they may be less enlightened than some ancient Hebrews in recognizing the humanizing values of sexual relations. Many students view erotic love not as something elevating but as something they "fall into." They unwittingly follow the medieval monks who believed that the "Fall" of mankind resulted from succumbing to sexual temptation. Like Francis of Assisi, many speak depreciatingly of the part of the body where their genitals are located as their "ass."[27] Sex belongs to the smutty, pornographic cellar of life, which they think ought to be kept locked whenever authority figures are looking. Believing sex to be a devilish urge, they try to keep it separate from other parts of their personality. When desire for pleasure arises, they indulge anyway, assuming that love is something not necessarily associated with a long-term, well-rounded relationship. A divided personality and its accompanying guilt feelings are the inevitable results, and the goodness of a future whole marriage relationship is obscured.

The church, at national and congregational levels, needs to do much more in its ministry to youth. An auspicious start can be seen in those denominations which have endorsed positions associating sex with the sacred. The United Presbyterians, for example, have stated that human sexuality "is truly a vehicle of the spirit and a means of communion."[28] Denominational positions need to percolate down to particular congregations by means of good curriculum material for the church school. These questions also need to be considered: Do communicants classes associate the bodily with becoming a communing member of the body of Christ? Does the church provide enjoyable activities for its youth that can serve as a laboratory in *agapē?* Does the minister's counsel with engaged couples result in a lowering of somatic phobia and a heightened association of sex with what is *tob?*

This book has many implications for common worship, the time set apart by the church for its fullest expression of communion with God. Where in our society today is there to be found less authentic expression of emotion, or fewer pleasurable sensations, than in the usual Sunday morning worship service? The bolted-down pew of

main-line denominations symbolizes the triumph of stultifying con-
formity over exuberant spontaneity: the worshiper who wiggles more
than his toes is considered to be out of order. Our sitting-room
sanctuaries afford a tame and devitalized experience in comparison
with the dance floor, the universal place of worship in man's not-too-
distant past.

Sam Keen charges that Protestants tend to believe that "the ear
is the organ of salvation," for "healing comes not from what may be
seen, or felt, or touched but from *hearing* the word of God."[29] As
one who was also reared as a Southern Presbyterian, I share Keen's
self-criticism. The sanctuary experience in many churches composed
of white, educated Protestants is indeed largely a matter of listening
to and looking at performers with varying degrees of expertise. It is
like a fancy diving performance, where the onlookers miss the exhila-
ration of feeling the arms and legs moving in rhythm, and the in-
vigorating sensations of the plunge into the water. Even in the choir,
physical movement is mostly confined to the larynx, in spite of the
fact that the term "choir" comes from *choros*, which originally de-
noted a band of dancer-singers.

The charismatic movement is a valid protest against the current
dominant mode of Christian worship. Pentecostals recognize that
worship services in the first century were not centered in monologues
by persons trained in oratory. They know that Paul asked each worshiper to contribute something that might edify the community (I
Cor. 14:26). Pentecostals are more actors than auditors, and their
services contain considerable body language. The mushrooming
growth of their numbers in many parts of the globe may be due in
part to their acceptance of spontaneous dance as an act of praise.[30]
However, it would be unwise to swap the nonsense babble of some
"glossolaliacs" for the non-sense hyperintellectualism of some
churches. Following Paul, I think that there is a midpoint between
the static and the ecstatic poles of worship, where both rational
dialogue and emotional release can be unified.

Suggestions for the improvement of stultifying worship services
that have already been made in this book include the use of interpretive dance, sensuous liturgies, and sacramental meals. Youth choirs
have begun singing rock operas, such as *Jesus Christ Superstar* and

Godspell, which more adequately express some authentic aspects of the sensuousness of Biblical persons. Since a key factor in the desensitizing of worship services has been the lack of participation by all the members of the group, churches should direct primary attention to correcting this problem. Smaller groups, informal worship "in-the-round," and neighborhood house meetings have been found to be effective approaches. The house church, which was the setting for all worship during the first centuries of church history, is now receiving more attention as we begin to grow out of our edifice complex, and this is a hopeful sign. Participation by many individuals in preparing for the service is a key to providing both exuberant and meaningful spontaneity when the group comes together.

All the bodily senses should celebrate the divine immanence. The person who is faithful to Biblical religion is the very opposite of the killjoy. He or she should be seen as one who resurrects joy in such common activities as eating, drinking, dancing, and making love. As humans and not angels, we should not prepare for God's revelation by singing the old hymn, "Let sense be dumb, let flesh retire." Rather, we should sing a new song: "Let sense awake, let flesh revive." That motif was prominent among the Israelites, and it is treated in their best-loved hymn. A psalmist spoke of the Lord in words that may be translated:

> He makes me lie down in green pastures
> and leads me to refreshing waters.
> He resensitizes my whole self![31]
> (Ps. 23:2–3a)

Along with the down-to-earth Hebrews and the early Christians, our doxology is to "God, who generously gives us everything to enjoy" (I Tim. 6:17). May this book serve to effect more harmonious vibrations between profound human and divine love, between the spirited body and the Spirit of God.

Notes

INTRODUCTION

1. Jacques Maritain, *Moral Philosophy* (New York, 1964), p. 454.

2. "Interview with Marshall McLuhan," *The Review of Books and Religion*, Vol. 3, Mid-June 1974, p. 2.

3. Quoted in John Scopes, "The Trial That Rocked the Nation," *Reader's Digest*, Vol. 78, March 1961, p. 141.

4. Michael Novak, *Ascent of the Mountain, Flight of the Dove* (New York, 1971), p. 25.

5. Rollo May, *Love and Will* (New York, 1969), p. 45.

6. Cf. Isa. 31:3; Johannes Pedersen, *Israel* (London, 1926–1940), Vol. I-II, p. 176.

7. Cf. Otto J. Baab, *The Theology of the Old Testament* (New York, 1949), pp. 108, 110, 226.

8. William Temple, *Nature, Man, and God* (London, 1935), p. 478.

9. Norman Brown, *Love's Body* (New York, 1966), p. 222.

10. Phil. 3:21. That "lowly" is the proper adjective here can be seen by examining the use of the same term in Luke 1:48; cf. William E. Phipps, *Was Jesus Married?* (New York, 1970), pp. 99–119.

11. Rudolf Bultmann, *Theology of the New Testament* (New York, 1951), p. 194; cf. Phil. 1:20; Rom. 12:1; John A. T. Robinson, *The Body: A Study in Pauline Theology* (Chicago, 1952), p. 14.

12. Edward Gibbon, *The Decline and Fall of the Roman Empire* 15. 4.

13. Friedrich Nietzsche, *The Genealogy of Morals* 3. 2.

Chapter 1. DANCE AND RELIGION

1. Basil Davidson, *African Kingdoms* (New York, 1971), p. 148.

2. Cf. James G. Frazer, *The Golden Bough* (New York, 1960), pp. 30–32, 73–74, 136–146, 495–496, 706–730; Curt Sachs, *World History of the Dance* (New York, 1937), pp. 207–248.

3. "Dance, Japanese," *Encyclopaedia Britannica* (Chicago, 1970).

4. *Rig Veda* 10. 72; cf. Egon Wellesz (ed.), *Ancient and Oriental Music* (London, 1957), p. 204.

5. Cf. Ananda Coomaraswamy (tr.), *The Mirror of Gesture* (New Delhi, 1970); Ruth Reyna, *Introduction to Indian Philosophy* (Bombay, 1971), pp. 232–233.

6. Aristotle, *Poetics* 4; cf. Jane E. Harrison, *Themis* (Cambridge, 1912), p. 43.

7. Aristophanes, *Frogs* 332–335.

8. Euripides, *Bacchae* 23–24.

9. Homer, *Odyssey* 8. 260–264; 12. 318; cf. Edward A. Lippman, *Musical Thought in Ancient Greece* (New York, 1964), p. 54.

10. Cf. Dorothy K. Hill, *The Dance in Classical Times* (Baltimore, 1945).

11. Friedrich Nietzsche, *Thus Spake Zarathustra* 1. 7.

12. Gerardus van der Leeuw, *Sacred and Profane Beauty* (New York, 1963), pp. 74, 331.

13. Cf. Otto Jespersen, *Language: Its Nature, Development and Origin* (London, 1922), p. 440; Susanne K. Langer, *Philosophy in a New Key*, 3d ed. (Cambridge, 1957), pp. 128–133; Frank B. Livingstone, "Did Australopithecines Sing?" *Current Anthropology*, Vol. 14 (1973), pp. 25–29.

14. Van der Leeuw, *Sacred and Profane Beauty*, p. 297.

15. Cf. "Dance," *Encyclopaedia Judaica* (Jerusalem, 1971).

16. An Egyptian wall carving of the same dynastic period as the exodus shows women dancing with tambourines and castanets. See James B. Pritchard, *The Ancient Near East in Pictures* (Princeton, 1954), p. 66.

17. Judg. 21:21, 23; Mishnah, *Taanith* 4. 8; Josephus, *Antiquities* 5. 2. 12; Cf. Jer. 31:4–5.

18. Emil Hirsch, "Dance," *The Jewish Encyclopedia* (New York, 1903). On the original meaning of ḥag as "round dance," see J. Morgenstern, "The Etymological History of the Three Hebrew

Synonyms for 'to dance,' HGG, HLL and KRR, and their Cultural Significance," *American Oriental Society Journal* 36 (1916), p. 323.

19. Cf. D. Harvey, "Joy," *The Interpreter's Dictionary of the Bible* (New York, 1962).

20. Cf. Sigmund Mowinckel, *The Psalms in Israel's Worship* (New York, 1962), Vol. I, p. 11.

21. Ps. 118:27; cp. Ps. 26:6; 48:12; W. O. E. Oesterley, *The Sacred Dance* (Cambridge, 1923), p. 92; Roland de Vaux, *Ancient Israel* (New York, 1965), Vol. II, p. 512; Artur Weiser, *The Psalms* (Philadelphia, 1962), p. 729.

22. Louis M. Epstein, *Sex Laws and Customs in Judaism* (New York, 1948), pp. 92, 102.

23. W. Robertson Smith, *The Religion of the Semites* (New York, 1957), p. 254.

24. J. Millar, "Dance," in James Hastings (ed.), *Dictionary of the Bible* (Edinburgh, 1898–1904).

25. Oesterley, *The Sacred Dance*, p. 34.

26. Johannes Lindblom, *Prophecy in Ancient Israel* (Philadelphia, 1962), p. 59.

27. Mowinckel, *The Psalms in Israel's Worship*, Vol. I, p. 10.

28. Alfred Guillaume, *Prophecy and Divination* (London, 1938), pp. 298–299; cf. Alfred Haldar, *Associations of Cult Prophets Among the Ancient Semites* (Uppsala, 1945), p. 119.

29. II Sam. 6:16; Hans W. Hertzberg, *I and II Samuel* (Philadelphia, 1964), p. 28.

30. Cf. Heliodorus, *Aethiopica* 4. 17; Roland de Vaux, "Les Prophètes de Baal sur le mont Carmel," *Bulletin du Musée de Beyrouth*, Vol. 5 (1941), pp. 9–11; John Gray, *I and II Kings* (Philadelphia, 1963), p. 353.

31. Apuleius, *The Golden Ass* 8. 27–28; cf. Frazer, *The Golden Bough* (New York, 1960), p. 405.

32. James B. Pritchard (ed.), *Ancient Near Eastern Texts* (Princeton, 1955), p. 142.

33. Cf. Pedersen, *Israel*, Vol. III–IV, p. 470.

34. *Sukkah* 4, 5.

35. Cf. Louis Finkelstein, *The Pharisees* (Philadelphia, 1966), pp. 102–103.

36. Socrates, *Church History* 7. 13.

37. Israel Abrahams, *Jewish Life in the Middle Ages* (New York, 1958), p. 380.

38. "Dance," *Encyclopaedia Judaica.*

39. E.g., Jer. 7:34; S. of Songs 6:13. K. Rexroth, in *Saturday Review*, April 29, 1969, p. 16, argues that "the Song of Songs is a collection of dance lyrics for group marriage."

40. E.g., Job 41:22. Matthew Black, in *An Aramaic Approach to the Gospels and Acts* (Oxford, 1954), p. 271, argues cogently that *duts* is behind the verbs *skirtēsate* in Luke 6:23 and *agalliasthe* in Matt. 5:12. The verb *agallian* is also used in Luke 10:21.

41. *Sukkah* 4, 5.

42. Plato, *Laws* 654.

43. Mark 14:26; Matt. 26:30. The Hebrew word for Passover *(pesach)* may have originally connoted a spring dance, for a verb with the same root is used in I Kings 18:26 to refer to a ritual dance.

44. *Pesahim* 10. 7; cf. Gustaf Dalman, *Jesus-Jeshua* (New York, 1971), pp. 131–132.

45. *Acts of John* 94–97.

46. Cf. Lucien Deiss, *Dancing for God* (Cincinnati, 1969), p. 7.

47. E.g., Homer, *Odyssey* 2. 12; cf. "Grace," in James Hastings (ed.), *Encyclopaedia of Religion and Ethics* (Edinburgh, 1908–1921).

48. Harvey Cox, *The Feast of Fools* (Cambridge, Mass., 1969), pp. 52, 54.

49. Lillian B. Lawler, *The Dance in Ancient Greece* (Middletown, Conn., 1964), p. 98.

50. Lucian, *The Dance* 15.

51. Clement of Alexandria, *Exhortation to the Greeks* 12.

52. Hippolytus, *Sermons on Passover* 6.

53. Gregory of Nazianzus, *Against Julian* 2; *Orations* 5. 35.

54. Gregory of Nyssa, *Sermons on Ecclesiastes* 6. 4.

55. John Chrysostom, *Sermon of Lazarus* 1; *Concerning the Statues* 19. 1; cf. E. Louis Backman, *Religious Dances* (London, 1952), p. 32.

56. Chrysostom, *Sermons on Matthew* 48. 4; cf. "Dance," *Dictionary of Christian Antiquities* (London, 1880).

57. Chrysostom, *Sermons on Colossians* 12.

58. Eusebius, *History of the Church* 10. 9.

59. *Ibid.*, 2. 17.

60. Philo, *On a Contemplative Life* 11.

61. Theodoret, *Church History* 3. 22.

62. Backman, *Religious Dances*, pp. 38–39.

63. Cf. Backman, *Religious Dances*, p. 11.

64. Lincoln Kirstein, *Dance* (New York, 1969), p. 40.

65. Sachs, *World History of Dance*, pp. 245–248.

66. Cf. Will Durant, *Caesar and Christ* (New York, 1944), p. 379.

67. Cicero, *Pro Murena* 6.

68. Russell M. Hughes, *Dance as an Art-Form* (New York, 1935), p. 24.

69. Ambrose, *Concerning Virgins* 3. 5.

70. Ambrose, *Concerning Repentance* 2. 41–43.

71. Augustine, *Confessions* 6. 6.

72. *Ibid.*, 10. 50.

73. Augustine, *Sermons* 326. 1.

74. *Ibid.*, 311. 5–7.

75. Augustine, *On the Psalms* 32. 2. 6.

76. E.g., edicts of the Council of Toledo (590) and the Trullan Synod (692); Backman, *Religious Dances*, pp. 35, 155–156; "Dance" in Percy A. Scholes (ed.), *The Oxford Companion to Music* (London, 1956).

77. Eileen Power, *Medieval People* (London, 1937), p. 83.

78. Dom Gougaud, "La Danse dans les églises," *Revue d'Histoire Ecclésiastique*, Vol. 15 (1914), p. 245.

79. Jacques Maritain, *Art and Scholasticism* (New York, 1962), p. 68. Also, Robert H. Benson, in *Papers of a Parish* (New York, 1907), pp. 106–126, finds ballet analogies in the expressive movements of the mass.

80. G. G. Coulton, *Five Centuries of Religion* (Cambridge, 1923), Vol. I, p. 531; cf. Backman, *Religious Dances*, pp. 44–327.

81. Cf. Kirstein, *Dance*, p. 91.

82. Cf. "Carole" and "Chorea" in Willi Apel, *Harvard Dictionary of Music*, 2d ed. (Cambridge, Mass., 1969); Suzanne Aker, "To Carol Is to Dance," *Dance Magazine*, Vol. 38 (Dec. 1964), p. 40.

83. Quoted in Margaret Fisk Taylor, *A Time to Dance* (Philadelphia, 1967), p. 117.

84. Kirstein, *Dance*, p. 133.

85. "Seises," *Harvard Dictionary of Music*.

86. Jehan Tabourot, *Orchesography* (1589; New York, 1948), pp. 12–13.

87. William Tyndale, *Prologue to the New Testament* (1525).

88. Cf. Will Durant, *The Reformation* (New York, 1957), p. 419; Preserved Smith, *The Age of the Reformation* (New York, 1920), p. 500.

89. *Luthers Werke* (Berlin, 1962), Vol. VIII, p. 283 (Table Talk, No. 5265).

90. *D. Martin Luthers Werke* (Weimar, 1927), Vol. VIII, Part 2, p. 64.

91. Cf. Roland H. Bainton, *Here I Stand* (New York, 1955), p. 226.

92. John Calvin, *Commentaries,* Library of Christian Classics, Vol. XXIII (Philadelphia, 1958), p. 355 (on Gen. 4:21); cf. van der Leeuw, *Sacred and Profane Beauty,* p. 52.

93. See John Calvin, *Theological Treatises,* Library of Christian Classics, Vol. XXII (Philadelphia, 1954), p. 81.

94. Percy A. Scholes, *The Puritans and Music* (New York, 1962), p. 340.

95. John Calvin, *The First Epistle of Paul the Apostle to the Corinthians* (Grand Rapids, 1960), p. 159.

96. Larger Catechism, q. 139.

97. Scholes, *The Puritans and Music,* p. 144.

98. John Milton, *L'Allegro* 33–34.

99. *Ibid.,* 91–98.

100. John Bunyan, *The Pilgrim's Progress* (Philadelphia, 1891), p. 244.

101. Scholes, *The Puritans and Music,* p. 132.

102. *Ibid.,* p. 69; cf. Kirstein, *Dance,* pp. 330–331.

103. Henry B. Parkes, *Jonathan Edwards* (New York, 1930), p. 28.

104. Margaret Fisk Taylor, *A Time to Dance,* p. 121.

105. Quoted in Edward D. Andrews, *The People Called Shakers* (New York, 1953), pp. 140–141.

106. Marcus Bach, *Strange Sects and Curious Cults* (New York, 1961), p. 214.

107. Edward D. Andrews, *The Gift to Be Simple* (Locust Valley, N.Y., 1940), p. 17.

108. Cf. C. Green and S. Wells, *A Summary View of the Millennial Church* (Albany, N.Y., 1823), pp. 80–85.

109. Cf. *Time,* June 22, 1959, p. 47. For the quotation from Joseph Smith, see his *The Doctrine and Covenants of the Church of Jesus Christ of Latter Day Saints* 136. 28.

110. Wallace F. Bennett, *Why I Am a Mormon* (Boston, 1958), p. 139.

111. Cf. LeRoi Jones, *Blues People* (New York, 1963), pp. 43–44.

112. Quoted from *The Nation*, May 30, 1867, in H. E. Krehbiel, *Afro-American Folksongs* (New York, 1914), p. 33.

113. John Wesley, *Journal* (London, 1909), Vol. I, p. 19.

114. "Amusements" in Matthew Simpson, *Cyclopaedia of Methodism* (Philadelphia, 1882).

115. J. T. Crane, *Popular Amusements* (New York, 1869), pp. 99, 102–103.

116. Quoted in J. H. Brookes, *May Christians Dance?* (New York, 1869), pp. 89, 110–111, 127.

117. James Russell Lowell, "A Fable for Critics" in *Complete Poetical Works* (Boston, 1896), p. 126.

118. Cf. Ernest T. Thompson, *Presbyterians in the South*, Vols. II–III (Richmond, Va., 1973), Vol. II, pp. 392–397; Vol. III, p. 231.

119. "Amusements," *Encyclopedia of Southern Baptists* (Nashville, 1958); cf. R. C. Campbell, *Modern Evils* (New York, 1933), pp. 41–42.

120. "Recreation and Amusements" in *Seventh-Day Adventist Encyclopedia* (Washington, 1966).

121. Stewart Headlam, in *Church Reformer*, Oct. 1884.

122. Cf. van der Leeuw, *Sacred and Profane Beauty*, p. 30; G. R. S. Mead, "The Sacred Dance of Jesus," *The Quest* (Oct. 1910), pp. 45–67.

123. Cf. W. Sandys, *Christmas Carols* (London, 1833), pp. 110–112; *The Oxford Book of Carols* (London, 1928), no. 71.

124. T. Arnold (ed.), *Select English Works of John Wyclif* (Oxford, 1869–1871), Vol. III, p. 360.

125. Cf. Margaret Fisk Taylor, *A Time to Dance*, p. 128; Andrews, *The Gift to Be Simple*, p. 136.

126. Cp. John 11:25–26; 12:32; 15:4. "Lord of the Dance" can be found in D. Kell (ed.), *Hymns for Now*, Vol. I (Chicago, 1967).

127. Ted Shawn, "Religious Use of Dance," in F. Ernest Johnson (ed.), *Religious Symbolism* (New York, 1955), pp. 146–156.

128. Margaret Fisk, *The Art of the Rhythmic Choir* (New York, 1950); Margaret Fisk Taylor, *A Time to Dance; idem, Creative Movement* (New York, 1969); cf. Violet Bruce and Joan Tooke, *Lord of the Dance: An Approach to Religious Education* (London, 1966).

129. Margaret Fisk Taylor, *A Time to Dance*, p. 8.

130. Doug Adams, *Congregational Dancing in Christian Worship* (Vallejo, Calif., 1971).

131. Cf. *Time*, May 17, 1968, p. 80.

132. Deiss, *Dancing for God*, p. 5.

133. John Killinger, *Leave It to the Spirit* (New York, 1971), pp. 38, 63–64.

Chapter 2. THE PLIGHT OF THE SONG OF SONGS

1. Cf. James B. Pritchard (ed.), *Ancient Near Eastern Texts*, pp. 468–469; Theophile J. Meek, "Babylonian Parallels to the Song of Songs," *Journal of Biblical Literature*, Vol. 43 (1924), pp. 245–252.

2. John Milton, *Of Education* 6. In Milton's definition, poetry is "simple, sensuous, and passionate."

3. Theophile J. Meek, "The Song of Songs, Introduction," *The Interpreter's Bible*, Vol. V (New York, 1956), p. 91.

4. Cf. Gen. 29:27; Judg. 14:17.

5. *Sotah* 9. 14.

6. Cf. Tobit 7:16; 8:4.

7. Jerusalem *Kiddushin* 2. 65d.

8. Robert Browning, "Rabbi Ben Ezra" 71–72.

9. *Taanith* 4. 8.

10. Tosephta *Sanhedrin* 12. 10.

11. *Sifra* on Lev. 19:18.

12. *Yadaim* 3. 5.

13. Philo, *The Migration of Abraham* 89–94; cf. *allēgoreō* in G. Kittel (ed.), *Theological Dictionary of the New Testament*, Vol. I (Grand Rapids, 1964).

14. R. P. C. Hanson, *Allegory and Event* (London, 1959), p. 25; cf. *Shabbath* 63a.

15. See Christian D. Ginsburg, *The Song of Songs* (London, 1857).

16. Abraham ben Isaac ha-Levi, *Commentary on the Song of Songs* (Assen, 1970), p. 51.

17. Israel Abrahams, *Jewish Life in the Middle Ages* (New York, 1958), p. 163.

18. Origen, *Contra Celsus* 1. 17; cf. J. Tate, "The Beginnings of Greek Allegory," *Classical Review*, 1927, p. 214.

19. Cf. Eduard Zeller, *The Stoics, Epicureans, and Sceptics*, rev. ed. (New York, 1962), pp. 354–369.

20. Jean Leclercq, *The Love of Learning and the Desire for God* (New York, 1961), p. 106; cf. John C. Moore, *Love in Twelfth-Century France* (Philadelphia, 1972), pp. 36–38.

21. Cf. Hanson, *Allegory and Event*, pp. 116–117.

22. Origen, *Homilies on the Song of Songs* 1.

23. Origen, *Commentary on the Song of Songs* 3. 9.

24. *Ibid.*, 1. 4.

25. Plato, *Symposium* 180–185.

26. Origen, *Homilies on the Song of Songs* 1. 2.

27. Cf. James G. Frazer, *The Golden Bough* (London, 1955), Vol. II, pp. 135–143.

28. Adolf Harnack, *History of Dogma* (New York, 1961), Vol. II, p. 295.

29. Cf. Edgar Hennecke, *New Testament Apocrypha*, ed. by Wilhelm Schneemelcher (Philadelphia, 1965), Vol. II, pp. 432, 442.

30. Acts of Thomas 12–14.

31. *Ibid.*, 83, 98, 117, 124.

32. Jerome, *Letters* 80. 1.

33. *Ibid.*, 22. 25.

34. *Ibid.*, 107. 12.

35. Jerome, *Against Jovinian* 1. 20.

36. Jerome, *Letters* 22. 41; cp. S. of Songs 2:10.

37. Gregory of Nyssa, *Commentary on the Song of Songs* 14.

38. *Ibid.*, 10.

39. Ambrose, *Letters* 41. 14.

40. Ambrose, *On the Mysteries* 7. 39.

41. Ambrose, *Concerning Virgins* 1. 9. 49–51.

42. Ambrose, *On the Mysteries* 9. 58.

43. Ambrose, *On the Holy Spirit* 2. 5. 38.

44. Bernard of Clairvaux, *Sermons on the Song of Songs* 61.

45. *Ibid.*, 26.

46. *Ibid.*, 83.

47. William of St. Thierry, *Life of Bernard* 1. 3.

48. Horace, *Letters* 10. 24.

49. Abelard, *Ethics (Know Thyself)* 3.

50. Cf. Jeffrey G. Sikes, *Peter Abailard* (New York, 1965), pp. 223–224.

51. Bernard of Clairvaux, *Letters* 239; Cf. S. of Songs 2:15; Bernard of Clairvaux, *Sermons on the Song of Songs* 64.

52. Augustine, *On Christian Doctrine* 2. 6.

53. Sikes, *Peter Abailard*, pp. 222–224, 235.

54. Bernard of Clairvaux, *Sermons on the Song of Songs* 66. 12.

55. Quoted in Henry Adams, *Mont-Saint-Michel and Chartres* (Boston, 1933), pp. 313–314.

56. Arthur C. McGiffert, *A History of Christian Thought* (New York, 1933), Vol. II, p. 233.

57. Bernard of Clairvaux, *Sermons on the Song of Songs* 50. 7.

58. Bernard of Clairvaux, "Letter to the Bavarians," quoted in A. J. Luddy, *Life and Teaching of St. Bernard* (Dublin, 1927), p. 528.

59. Bernard of Clairvaux, *Letters* 399 (To Pope Eugenius III).

60. Cf. Denis de Rougemont, *Love in the Western World* (New York, 1956), pp. 243–271.

61. Dante, *Paradise* 31–33.

62. Richard S. Storrs, *Bernard of Clairvaux* (New York, 1912), p. 582.

63. Ray C. Petry (ed.), *Late Medieval Mysticism* (Philadelphia, 1957), p. 47.

64. Bernard Gui, *Life of St. Thomas Aquinas* 38.

65. E.g., R. E. Murphy, "Canticle of Canticles," *The Jerome Biblical Commentary* (Englewood Cliffs, N.J., 1969), p. 507.

66. See footnotes for the Song of Songs in *The Jerusalem Bible* (New York, 1966); see also *A New Catholic Commentary on Holy Scripture*, rev. ed. (London, 1969), sec. 426.

67. Quoted in Richard Friedenthal, *Luther: His Life and Times* (New York, 1970), pp. 65–66.

68. Jaroslav Pelikan (ed.), *Luther's Works*, Vol. XV (St. Louis, 1972), pp. 192–195.

69. *Ibid.*, p. 255.

70. Westminster Assembly, *Annotations Upon All the Books of the Old and New Testaments* (London, 1651), Vol. I (no pagination).

71. John Wesley, *Explanatory Notes Upon the Old Testament* (Bristol, 1765), Vol. III, p. 1926.

72. Jerome, *Against Jovinian* 1. 30.

73. Siricius, Letter to Himerius.

74. Henry B. Swete, *Theodori Episcopi Mopsuesteni in Epistolas Beati Pauli Commentarii*, Vol. I (Cambridge, 1880), pp. 73–79.

75. J. P. Migne (ed.), *Patrologia Graeca*, Vol. 66, p. 697.

76. Theodore of Mopsuestia, *On the Incarnation* 15.

77. Johannes Quasten, *Patrology* (Utrecht, 1966), Vol. III, p. 540.

78. Cf. A. Bea, *Canticum Canticorum Salomonis* (Rome, 1953), pp. 4–5.

79. John Calvin, *Commentaries on Galatians and Ephesians* (Edinburgh, 1854), pp. 135–136.

80. S. L. Greenslade (ed.), *The Cambridge History of the Bible*, Vol. II (Cambridge, 1963), p. 8.

81. John Calvin, *Commentary on the Book of Psalms* (Edinburgh, 1846), p. 173.

82. William Whiston, *A Supplement to Mr. Whiston's late Essay, towards the restoring the true text of the Old Testament, proving that the Canticles is not a Sacred Book of the Old Testament* (London, 1725), p. 5.

83. W. Ponsonby (ed.), *Complaints* (London, 1591), Preface. The translation is not extant.

84. E.g., Edmund Spenser, "The Faerie Queene" 2. 3. 28; 6. 8. 42; cp. S. of Songs 4:4; 5:15; Spenser, "Amoretti," sonnets 15 and 77; cp. S. of Songs 4:11; 5:11–15; cf. Israel Baroway, "The Imagery of Spenser and the Song of Songs," *Journal of English and Germanic Philology*, Vol. 33 (1934), pp. 23–45.

85. Edmund Spenser, "Epithalamion" 25, 171–180; cp. S. of Songs 2:12; 4:3; 7:1–4.

86. Spenser, "Epithalamion," 246, 249.

87. Johann G. von Herder, *Lieder der Liebe, die ältesten und schönsten aus dem Morgenlande* (Leipzig, 1778), pp. 89–106.

88. Johann W. von Goethe, "Westöstlicher Diwan" in *Werke* (Weimar, 1888), Vol. VII, p. 8.

89. H. H. Rowley, *The Servant of the Lord and Other Essays on the Old Testament* (Oxford, 1965), pp. 243, 245.

90. Dora Russell, *The Right to Be Happy* (New York, 1927), p. 128.

91. Herman Wouk, *This Is My God* (New York, 1959), p. 155; cf. William E. Phipps, *The Sexuality of Jesus* (New York, 1973), pp. 79–84.

92. McGiffert, *A History of Christian Thought*, Vol. I, p. 291; cf. Frederic W. Farrar, *The History of Interpretation* (New York, 1886), pp. 210–218.

93. Bernard of Clairvaux, *Sermons on the Song of Songs* 83. 4.

94. Bernard of Clairvaux, *On the Love of God* 15.

95. Claude Tresmontant, *A Study of Hebrew Thought* (New York, 1960), p. 93.

96. See *astorgoi* in Rom. 1:31 and in II Tim. 3:3; cp. *stergein* in I Clement 1:3.

97. Dietrich Bonhoeffer, *Letters and Papers from Prison* (New York, 1962), letters of May 20 and April 30, 1944.

Chapter 3. ASPECTS OF JESUS' PERSONALITY

1. Walt Whitman, "Song of Myself" 24.

2. Sigmund Freud, *Wit and Its Relation to the Unconscious* (New York, 1916), pp. 226–245.

3. Basil, *Ascetic Works*, Long Rules 17; John Chrysostom, *Sermons on Matthew* 6. 9; *Sermons on the Statues* 20. 23.

4. Ignatius Loyola, *Spiritual Exercises* 80; cp. *The Rule of St. Benedict* 7.

5. John Northbrooke, *A Treatise Against Dicing, Dancing, Plays and Interludes, with Other Idle Pastimes* (London, 1843), p. 179.

6. Herbert Asbury, *A Methodist Saint* (New York, 1927), p. 265.

7. Merton P. Strommen *et al.*, *A Study of Generations* (Minneapolis, 1972), p. 367; compare with Basil, who asserts that Jesus never laughed.

8. Friedrich Nietzsche, *Thus Spake Zarathustra* 1. 21; 4. 13. 20.

9. Elton Trueblood, *The Humor of Christ* (New York, 1964); J. Jonsson, *Humor and Irony in the New Testament* (Reykjavik, 1965).

10. George Bach and Peter Wyden, *The Intimate Enemy* (New York, 1969), p. 17.

11. Gordon Allport, *The Nature of Prejudice* (Boston, 1954), p. 497.

12. Thomas Aquinas, *Summa Theologica* 1–2. q. 84. 4.

13. Seneca, *On Anger* 1. 1, 12; 2. 10; 3. 6.

14. William Blake, "Auguries of Innocence."

15. Theodore Roszak, *Where the Wasteland Ends* (New York, 1972), p. 458.

16. Henry D. Thoreau, *A Week on the Concord and Merrimack Rivers*, p. 342.

17. Max Weber, *The Protestant Ethic and the Spirit of Capitalism* (New York, 1958), pp. 157, 119.

18. Leslie Rutledge, *Jesus' Teachings and the Use of Leisure* (1931), p. 12.

19. Cf. Fung Yu-lan, *A Short History of Chinese Philosophy* (New York, 1962), p. 138.

20. Aristotle, *Metaphysics* 986a.

21. Euripides, *Andromache* 181; *Phoenician Maidens* 197.

22. Philo, *On the Creation* 165.

23. See Sigmund Freud, "Lecture on Femininity" (1938); and see Erich Fromm, *The Art of Loving* (New York, 1963), pp. 31, 35.

24. Emil Brunner, *Man in Revolt* (Philadelphia, 1947), pp. 352–354.

25. Cf. "Sex," *The Interpreter's Dictionary of the Bible* (New York, 1962).

26. *Tao Te Ching* 28, 76.

27. Euripides, *Iphigenia Among the Tauri* 1058.

28. D. H. Parker (ed.), *Schopenhauer Selections* (New York, 1928), p. 437.

29. Aristotle, *History of Animals* 608b.

30. Juvenal, *Satires* 6. 273.

31. William Shakespeare, *Henry VIII* 3. 2. 428; *Macbeth* 4. 3. 230.

32. Lord Chesterfield, *Letters*, Sept. 5, 1748; Parker (ed.), *Schopenhauer Selections*, p. 436.

33. Luke 23:46; Ps. 31:5; Talmud, *Berakot* 5a.

34. Mary Carolyn Davies, "Door-Mats."

35. Henry Wadsworth Longfellow, "The Golden Legend" 2.

36. Aristotle, *Politics* 1254b-1260a.

37. Margaret Mead, *Sex and Temperament in Three Primitive Societies* (New York, 1935), p. 280.

38. Paul Mussen, "Early Sex-Role Development" in D. A. Goslin (ed.), *Handbook of Socialization Theory and Research* (Chicago, 1969), pp. 707–729.

39. Naomi Weisstein, "Psychology Constructs the Female" in A. Koedt (ed.), *Radical Feminism* (New York, 1973), pp. 189–196; Sidney Cornelia Callahan, *The Illusion of Eve* (New York, 1965), pp. 13–33, 78.

40. Cf. Lucy Komisar, *The New Feminism* (New York, 1971), p. 176.

41. "Campaign Teardrops," *Time*, Mar. 13, 1972, p. 20; Cf. *The New York Times*, Mar. 5, 1972, p. 33.

42. Sarah Grimke, *Letters on the Equality of the Sexes* (Boston, 1838), p. 18.

43. Theodore Roszak and Betty Roszak (eds.), *Masculine/Feminine* (New York, 1969), p. 102.

44. II Clement 12:2.

45. Gospel of Thomas 22, 114.

46. So Julius Cassianus, according to Clement of Alexandria, *Miscellanies* 3. 91–93.

47. Cf. Heinrich Zimmer, *Philosophies of India* (New York, 1951), pp. 5–8.

178

Chapter 4. SACRAMENTAL SEXUALITY

1. Origen, *Orations* 31. 4; *Ezekiel Selections* 7. Cp. regulations at Greek temples of the same era, which required abstinence from marital coitus for from one to three days before worship. Cf. Arthur D. Nock, *Early Gentile Christianity and Its Hellenistic Background* (New York, 1964), p. 18.

2. Timothy of Alexandria, Canons 5 and 15.

3. Cf. Jerome, *Letters* 48. 15; Aquinas, *Summa Theologica* 3. q. 80. 7.

4. *Penitential of Theodore* 1. 12. 1.

5. *Catechism of the Council of Trent,* tr. by J. A. McHugh and C. J. Callan (New York, 1923), p. 248.

6. Alfred C. Kinsey *et al.*, *Sexual Behavior in the Human Male* (Philadelphia, 1949), p. 482.

7. *Kethuboth* 62b.

8. *Zohar* 1. 50a.

9. Quoted in David Feldman, *Birth Control in Jewish Law* (New York, 1968), p. 102.

10. Augustine, *First Catechetical Instruction* 26. 50.

11. Dorothea Krook, *Three Traditions of Moral Thought* (Cambridge, 1959), p. 346.

12. William F. Arndt and F. Wilbur Gingrich, *A Greek-English Lexicon of the New Testament and Other Early Christian Literature* (Chicago, 1957).

13. Havelock Ellis, *Little Essays of Love and Virtue* (London, 1922), pp. 132–133.

14. Likewise, in the Old Testament, the same Hebrew term is employed in reference to "knowing" one's spouse sexually and "knowing" one's God.

15. David Mace, *The Christian Response to the Sexual Revolution* (Nashville, 1970), p. 133.

16. John Milton, *Paradise Lost* 8. 620–629.

17. Sidney Cornelia Callahan, *Beyond Birth Control: The Christian Experience of Sex* (New York, 1968), p. 54.

18. Paul Ricoeur, "Wonder, Eroticism, and Enigma," *Cross Currents,* 1964, p. 141.

19. Athenagoras, *A Plea Regarding Christians* 33.

20. W. Norman Pittenger, *The Christian Understanding of Human Nature* (Philadelphia, 1964), pp. 88, 92.

21. Phyllis Trible, "Depatriarchalizing in Biblical Interpretation," *Journal of the American Academy of Religion*, Vol. 41 (1973), p. 47.

22. E.g., Schalom Ben-Corin, *Bruder Jesus: Der Nazarener in jüdischer Sicht* (Munich, 1967), p. 129; Phipps, *Was Jesus Married?* also Frederick C. Grant, in *The Churchman*, Vol. 185 (Mar. 1971); Charles Davis, in *The Critic*, Vol. 30 (March-April 1972), pp. 57–60; Eugene Bianchi, in *National Catholic Reporter*, Vol. 10 (Sept. 13, 1974), p. 8.

23. Richard M. Langsdale, *The Sixth Jar* (New York, 1973), pp. 115, 141.

24. William Shakespeare, *Romeo and Juliet* 2. 2. 133–135.

25. Evgenii Lampert, *The Divine Realm* (London, 1943), pp. 97–98.

26. Michael Novak, "Closing the Gap between Theology and Marital Reality," *Commonweal*, Vol. 80 (1964), p. 344.

27. Michael Novak, *A Theology for Radical Politics* (New York, 1969), p. 104.

28. W. H. Auden, "For the Time Being: A Christmas Oratorio," *Collected Longer Poems* (New York, 1969), p. 197.

29. D. H. Lawrence, "A Propos of Lady Chatterley's Lover" in H. T. Moore (ed.), *Sex, Literature and Censorship* (New York, 1953), pp. 106–107.

30. Seward Hiltner, *Sex and the Christian Life* (New York, 1957), p. 61.

31. Martin Luther, *Babylonian Captivity of the Church* 6.

32. Walter Nigg, *The Heretics* (New York, 1962), p. 236.

33. Abraham Maslow, "Religion and Peak Experience," in John J. Heaney (ed.), *Psyche and Spirit* (New York, 1973), p. 97.

34. Andrew M. Greeley and William C. McCready, "Are We a Nation of Mystics?" *The New York Times Magazine*, Jan. 26, 1975, p. 22.

Chapter 5. AGAPĒ REVISITED

1. *Syntopicon of Great Books of the Western World* (Chicago, 1952), Vol. I, pp. 1060–1080; Mortimer Adler, *Great Ideas from the Great Books* (New York, 1961), p. 129.

2. Elizabeth Barrett Browning, "Sonnets from the Portuguese" 43.

3. Alvin Toffler, *Future Shock* (New York, 1971), p. 249.

4. Ceslaus Spicq, *Agape in the New Testament,* Vol. II (St. Louis, 1965), p. 80.

5. Karl Barth, *Church Dogmatics* (Edinburgh, 1958), IV/2, p. 740.

6. Denis de Rougemont, *Love in the Western World* (New York, 1956), pp. 71, 311.

7. Willard L. Sperry, *Jesus Then and Now* (New York, 1949), p. 130.

8. Pieter de Jong in John C. Wynn, (ed.), *Sex, Family, and Society in Theological Focus* (New York, 1966), p. 65.

9. Joseph Fletcher, *Situation Ethics* (Philadelphia, 1966), p. 103.

10. Thomas Gould, *Platonic Love* (New York, 1963), p. 18.

11. E.g., G. Johnston defines *agapē* as "passionless love" in "Love in the New Testament," *The Interpreter's Dictionary of the Bible;* cf. "Agape" in F. L. Cross (ed.), *The Oxford Dictionary of the Christian Church* (London, 1957); Arndt and Gingrich, *A Greek-English Lexicon of the New Testament and Other Early Christian Literature;* G. Abbott-Smith, *A Manual Greek Lexicon of the New Testament* (Edinburgh, 1937); Gerhard Kittel, *Lexicographia Sacra* (New York, 1938), pp. 19, 25–26. Usually no hint is given in lexicons that *agapē* and *agapan* are most commonly used in the Bible to refer to marital relations.

12. Anders Nygren, *Agape and Eros* (Philadelphia, 1953), pp. 210, 236.

13. *Ibid.,* p. 65.

14. See Nygren's essay in Charles W. Kegley (ed.), *The Philosophy and Theology of Anders Nygren* (Carbondale, Ill., 1970), pp. 358–365.

15. Cf. C. K. Barrett (ed.), *The New Testament Background* (New York, 1961), pp. 208–209.

16. Assumption of Moses 10:22.

17. *Manual of Discipline* 1. 10.

18. *Abodah Zarah* 2. 1.

19. Joseph Klausner, *Jesus of Nazareth* (New York, 1925), p. 376.

20. Edwin Markham, "Outwitted."

21. Walt Whitman, "You Felons on Trial in Courts."

22. David G. Flusser, *Jesus* (New York, 1969), p. 70. Jesus' love-the-enemy ethic is also distinctive vis à vis the pagan moral philosophy of the Greco-Roman civilization. Cf. Victor P. Furnish, *The*

Love Command in the New Testament (New York, 1972), p. 66.

23. Another verb, *philein*, is also employed, but it is used interchangeably with *agapan* as a synonym. Cf. James Moffatt, *Love in the New Testament* (New York, 1929), pp. 45–46.

24. Benjamin B. Warfield, "The Terminology of Love in the New Testament," *The Princeton Theological Review*, Vol. 16 (1918), pp. 182–183.

25. Robert Joly, *Le Vocabulaire chrétien de l'amour est-il original?* (Brussels, 1968), pp. 10–47.

26. Aristotle, *Nicomachean Ethics* 1124b.

27. Joseph Haroutunian, *God with Us* (Philadelphia, 1965), pp. 207–212.

28. Plato, *Symposium* 180–181.

29. Cf. G. M. A. Grube, *Plato's Thought* (Boston, 1958), pp. 115–117.

30. George Boas, "Love," *The Encyclopedia of Philosophy* (New York, 1967).

31. Richard Taylor, *Good and Evil* (New York, 1970), p. 229.

32. Diogenes Laërtius, *Lives of Eminent Philosophers* 7. 113.

33. Plotinus, *Enneads* 3. 5. 1–2.

34. José Ortega y Gasset, *On Love* (New York, 1957), p. 178.

35. Augustine, *Sermons on the Psalms* 31. 2. 5; 90. 1. 8; cf. Nygren, *Agape and Eros*, p. 500.

36. Søren Kierkegaard, *Works of Love* (Princeton, 1946), pp. 37–38, 46–47, 116.

37. William Lillie, *Studies in New Testament Ethics* (Philadelphia, 1961), pp. 177–178.

38. Paul Tillich, *Morality and Beyond* (New York, 1963), p. 42; cf. *idem.*, *Love, Power, and Justice* (New York, 1954), p. 5.

39. William G. Cole, *Sex and Love in the Bible* (New York, 1959), p. 22.

40. George F. Thomas, *Christian Ethics and Moral Philosophy* (New York, 1955), p. 79.

41. Dante, *Paradise* 33. 85.

42. *Selected Poems of Emily Dickinson* (New York, 1924), p. 50.

43. Cf., e.g., Martin Luther, *Theses for the Heidelberg Disputation* 28.

44. Reinhold Niebuhr, "Toward New Intra-Christian Endeavor," *The Christian Century*, Vol. 86 (1969), pp. 1664–1666.

Chapter 6. THE INTIMATE SENSES AND BEAUTY

1. Plato, *Greater Hippias* 297–299.

2. Cf. F. J. Kovach, "The Role of the Senses in the Aesthetic Experience," *Southwestern Journal of Philosophy*, Vol. 1 (Fall, 1970), pp. 91–102.

3. Augustine, *On Freedom of the Will* 2. 7, 14.

4. Aquinas, *Summa Theologica* 1–2. q. 27. 1; cf. Jacques Maritain, *Art and Scholasticism* (New York, 1962), p. 23.

5. Arthur Schopenhauer, *The World as Will and Idea* (London, 1883), Vol. II, p. 195; George Santayana, *The Sense of Beauty* (New York, 1896), p. 65.

6. Edmund Burke, *A Philosophical Enquiry Into the Origin of our Ideas of the Sublime and Beautiful* (1756), 3. 24, 26; Benedetto Croce, *Aesthetic* (New York, 1922), pp. 18–19, 82; cf. Helen Parkhurst, *Beauty* (New York, 1930), pp. 61–84.

7. Thomas Munro, *The Arts and Their Interrelations* (New York, 1949), p. 136.

8. André-Marie Dubarle, *Love and Fruitfulness in the Bible* (DePere, Wis., 1968), p. 46.

9. Phyllis Trible, "Depatriarchalizing in Biblical Interpretation," *Journal of the American Academy of Religion*, Vol. 41 (Mar. 1973), p. 44.

10. *Genesis Apocryphon* 20.

11. Helen Keller, "Sense and Sensibility," *The Century Magazine*, Vol. 75 (1908), pp. 566, 576–577.

12. Frances W. Herring, "Touch—the Neglected Sense," *The Journal of Aesthetics and Art Criticism*, Vol. 7 (Mar. 1949), p. 214.

13. See the apocalyptic *Sibylline Oracles* 3. 592–593; 4. 165; on the origin of the proverb, see John Bartlett, *Familiar Quotations* (Boston, 1968), p. 421.

14. *Leviticus Rabbah* 34. 3.

15. *Yoma* 3. 2.

16. *Abodah Zarah* 3. 4.

17. *Shabbath* 33b; *Sanhedrin* 17b.

18. "Bathing," *Universal Jewish Encyclopedia* (New York, 1948).

19. "Perfume," *The Interpreter's Dictionary of the Bible* (New York, 1962).

20. Roy Bedichek, *The Sense of Smell* (New York, 1960), p. 193.

21. John Milton, *Paradise Lost* 9. 192–197; see also book 5.

22. Keller, "Sense and Sensibility," *loc. cit.*, pp. 574, 783.

23. Josephus, *War* 2. 8. 3.

24. Cf. Athenaeus, *Deipnosophistae* 12. 78, 553; I Sam. 25:41.

25. Stanley Lane-Poole, *The Speeches and Table Talk of the Prophet Mohammed* (London, 1882), p. xxviii.

26. Carl Sandburg, "To a Contemporary Bunkshooter."

27. Athanasius, *Life of Anthony* 7.

28. *Ibid.*, 47, 60.

29. Cf. Herbert B. Workman, *The Evolution of the Monastic Ideal* (London, 1913), p. 64.

30. Jerome, *Letters* 45. 3–4; 108. 20.

31. *Ibid.*, 107. 11.

32. *Ibid.*, 125. 7.

33. Irenaeus, *Against Heresies* 3. 3. 4; cf. Jerome, *Prologue to the Gospel of John.*

34. Friedrich Nietzsche, *The Anti-Christ* 21.

35. James W. Thompson, *Economic and Social History of the Middle Ages* (New York, 1959), p. 431.

36. John Calvin, *Institutes* 3. 10. 2.

37. Theodore Roszak, *Where the Wasteland Ends,* p. 89.

38. Herbert A. Otto and John Mann (eds.), *Ways of Growth* (New York, 1968), p. 54.

39. E.g., Jerome, *Against Jovinian* 2. 6.

40. Athanasius, *Life of Anthony* 7, 45.

41. Jerome, *Letters* 54. 10; *Against Jovinian* 2. 7.

42. Augustine, *Confessions* 10. 44.

43. Bonaventura, *Life of St. Francis* 5. 1.

44. Calvin, *Institutes* 3. 10. 1.

45. Calvin, *Commentary on Genesis* 43:34.

46. E.g., Eccl. 8:15; Tobit 7:9. Luke 12:19 and 15:23 are two instances of the use of this saying in Jesus' parables. The rich fool is censured because he attempted to combine enjoyment with greed, whereas the prodigal's father is approved because of his attempt to combine enjoyment with forgiveness.

47. Norman Perrin, *The New Testament* (New York, 1974), p. 288.

48. Cf. J. F. Keating, *The Agape and the Eucharist in the Early Church* (London, 1901), p. 40.

49. Cf. *Berakoth* 6. 6–7; "The Agape," *The Interpreter's Dictionary of the Bible.*

50. Tertullian, *Apology* 39.

51. Augustine, *Confessions* 6. 2.

52. Augustine, *Letters* 29 (to Alypius).

53. Council of Laodicea (363); Trullan Synod (692), Canon 74.

54. Michael Novak, *Ascent of the Mountain, Flight of the Dove* (New York, 1970), p. 26.

55. *Christianity Today*, Oct. 26, 1973, p. 45.

56. Kahlil Gibran, *Jesus the Son of Man* (New York, 1928), pp. 79, 97.

57. William Wordsworth, "The Prelude" 12.

58. Calvin, *Institutes* 3. 10. 2–3.

59. Lawrence Meredith, *The Sensuous Christian* (New York, 1972), pp. 164–165.

60. Pierre Teilhard de Chardin, *The Divine Milieu* (New York, 1965), pp. 64, 105, 115.

Chapter 7. THE KISS OF LOVE

1. Ashley Montagu, *Touching* (New York, 1971), pp. 221, 264.

2. Aristotle, *On the Soul* 434b; *Nicomachean Ethics* 1169b.

3. Jane van Lawick-Goodall, *In the Shadow of Man* (Boston, 1971), p. 248.

4. Margaret Mead and James Baldwin, *A Rap on Race* (New York, 1971), pp. 45–47.

5. Rollo May, *Love and Will* (New York, 1969), pp. 16, 29, 303.

6. Julius Fast, *Body Language* (New York, 1970), p. 79.

7. Carl R. Rogers, "The Increasing Involvement of the Psychologist in Social Problems," *California State Psychologist*, Vol. 9 (1968), p. 29.

8. Quoted in Jane Howard, *Please Touch* (New York, 1970), p. 214.

9. *Kataphilein*, used in Luke 7:38, means "to kiss thoroughly."

10. Fyodor Dostoevsky, *The Brothers Karamazov* (New York, 1943), p. 322.

11. Clement of Alexandria, *Outlines* 7 as quoted in Eusebius, *Church History* 2. 9.

12. E.g., Ignatius, *Polycarp* 2. 3; Plutarch, *Life of Pericles* 1.

13. E.g., Frederick Field, *Notes on the Translation of the New Testament* (Cambridge, 1899), p. 34; Martin Dibelius, *From Tradi-*

tion to Gospel (London, 1934), p. 50n1; Dennis E. Nineham, *The Gospel of St. Mark* (New York, 1963), pp. 274–275.

14. George R. Potter and Evelyn M. Simpson (eds.), *The Sermons of John Donne* (Berkeley, 1957), Vol. III, p. 320.

15. Nicolas J. Perella, *The Kiss Sacred and Profane* (Berkeley, 1969), p. 15.

16. Greek, *philēma agapēs.*

17. James Moffatt, *The First Epistle of Paul to the Corinthians* (London, 1938), p. 280.

18. Justin Martyr, *Apology* 1. 65.

19. Tertullian, *Of Orations* 18; *To His Wife* 2. 4.

20. Cyprian, *Unity of the Catholic Church* 9.

21. Cyril of Jerusalem, *Catecheses* 23. 3; Matt. 5:23–24.

22. John Chrysostom, *Baptismal Instructions* 11; *Homilies on II Corinthians* 30.

23. Athenagoras, *A Plea Regarding Christians* 32–33.

24. Clement of Alexandria, *The Instructor* 3. 81, 12.

25. *Apostolic Constitutions* 2. 57.

26. *Penitential of Theodore* 1. 8. 1.

27. Geoffrey May, *Social Control of Sex Expression* (London, 1930), p. 28.

28. Cf. Clement of Alexandria, *Miscellanies* 6. 74, 105, 111; Workman, *The Evolution of the Monastic Ideal,* p. 37.

29. Plutarch, *Marriage Counsel* 12. Regarding Cato's contempt for private marital, as well as public, expression of sensual passion, see citation in Augustine, *On Marriage and Concupiscence* 1. 15. 17.

30. A. D. Nock in *The Cambridge Ancient History* Vol. XII (Cambridge, 1956), p. 449; A. C. Swinburne, "Hymn to Proserpine."

31. Josef A. Jungmann, *The Early Liturgy* (South Bend, Ind., 1959), p. 128.

32. Andrews, *The People Called Shakers,* p. 144.

33. *Time,* Aug. 21, 1968, p. 55; *The New York Times,* July 24, 1968, p. 3.

34. Orson Hyde, *Journal of Discources of Brigham Young,* Vol. IV (1857), p. 259.

35. Quoted in Thayer A. Greene, *Modern Man in Search of Manhood* (New York, 1967), p. 111.

36. Harvey Cox, *The Seduction of the Spirit* (New York, 1973), pp. 217–218.

37. Bernard Gunther, *Sense Relaxation Below Your Mind* (New York, 1968), p. 125.

Chapter 8. THE SENSUOUS SEMITIC PARADISE

1. Xenophon, *Anabasis* 1. 2. 7.
2. Josephus, *Against Apion* 1. 19.
3. Gerhard von Rad, *Genesis* (Philadelphia, 1961), p. 78.
4. Pritchard, *Ancient Near Eastern Texts*, pp. 38–44.
5. *Ibid.*, p. 95.
6. *Ibid.*, p. 89.
7. Walther Eichrodt, *Theology of the Old Testament*, Vol. I (Philadelphia, 1961), p. 480.
8. *Numbers Rabbah* 13. 2.
9. Papias, *Exposition of the Lord's Sayings* 4, as quoted in Irenaeus, *Against Heresies* 5. 33. 3.
10. Cf. C. H. Dodd, *The Interpretation of the Fourth Gospel* (Cambridge, 1958), pp. 144–150.
11. Cf. R. H. Charles, "Enoch, Book of the Secrets of," Hastings (ed.), *Dictionary of the Bible*.
12. *Numbers Rabbah* 13. 2; cf. S. of Songs 5:1.
13. Lactantius, *Divine Institutes* 7. 24.
14. *Patrologia Orientalis*, Vol. I, p. 1014.
15. Ephraim, *Hymns of Paradise* 3.
16. Tor Andrae, *Mohammed* (New York, 1960), pp. 87–88; R. V. C. Bodley, *The Messenger* (New York, 1969), p. 98.
17. Koran 7:31–32.
18. *Ibid.*, 5:1, 5; 16:14; 46:5–8.
19. *Ibid.*, 43:70.
20. *Ibid.*, 36:55.
21. *Ibid.*, 47:15.
22. *Ibid.*, 35:33–35.
23. *Ibid.*, 78:31–34.
24. *Ibid.*, 56:12–36.
25. *Ibid.*, 75:22–23.
26. *Ibid.*, 44:54; 52:20; 55:72; 56:22.
27. *Ibid.*, 2:25; 3:15.
28. Al-Tabari, *Tafsir* 27, as quoted in Andrae, *Mohammed*, p. 57.
29. Cf. A. J. Arberry, *Omar Khayyam* (New Haven, n.d.), pp. 102–103.

30. Omar Khayyám, *Rubáiyát* 12, 13.

31. Hesiod, *Works and Days* 169–173; cf. F. E. and F. P. Manuel, "Sketch for a Natural History of Paradise," *Daedalus*, Vol. 101 (Winter 1972), pp. 84–89.

32. Plato, *Republic* 363.

33. Origen, *First Principles* 2. 11. 6.

34. Augustine, *City of God*, 22. 30.

35. *Ibid.*, 13. 21.

36. Augustine, *On Christian Doctrine* 1. 4.

37. Augustine, *Confessions* 10. 6.

38. Cf. Aquinas, *Summa Theologica* 3. q. 81. 4; Dante, *Paradise*.

39. Tertullian, *The Shows* 30.

40. Aquinas, *Summa Theologica* 1–2. q. 67. 1; 3. q. 91. 5; 3. q. 94. 1.

41. Cf. Albert E. Bailey, *The Gospel in Hymns* (New York, 1950), pp. 277, 593.

42. "Jerusalem, My Happy Home," in John Julian, *A Dictionary of Hymnology*, 2d ed. (New York, 1957).

43. John Milton, *Paradise Lost* 4. 132, 217, 495–497, 505–507; 5. 304, 444–445; 4. 728.

44. John Milton, *Paradise Regained* 4. 587–589, 613–615.

45. Paul Tillich, *The Dynamics of Faith* (New York, 1957), pp. 42–43.

46. Mircea Eliade, *Patterns in Comparative Religion* (Cleveland, 1963), p. 433.

47. Cf. George F. Moore, *History of Religions*, Vol. II (New York, 1919), p. 399.

48. William M. Watt, *What Is Islam?* (New York, 1968), p. 230.

CONCLUSION

1. Havelock Ellis, *The Dance of Life* (Boston, 1923), pp. 36, 65–66.

2. Robert L. Short, *The Gospel According to Peanuts* (Richmond, Va., 1965), p. 112.

3. Hugo Rahner, *Man at Play* (New York, 1967), p. 87.

4. Jürgen Moltmann, *Theology of Play* (New York, 1972), p. 34.

5. Plato, *Phaedo* 65–67.

6. *Ibid.*, 68; Plato, *Symposium* 210–211.

7. Oscar Cullmann, "Immortality of the Soul or Resurrection of

the Dead?" in Krister Stendahl (ed.), *Immortality and Resurrection* (New York, 1965), p. 14.

8. Cf. Seneca, *Letters* 41. 2; 66. 12; 120. 14.

9. *Ibid.*, 65. 21.

10. Cf. Epictetus, *Discourses* 3. 15, 22; Marcus Aurelius, *Meditations* 8. 10.

11. Plotinus, *Enneads* 1. 2. 3; 1. 7. 3.

12. Basil, *On Reading Greek Literature* 9.

13. Josef Goldbrunner, *Holiness Is Wholeness and Other Essays* (South Bend, Ind., 1964), pp. 4–5.

14. Descartes, *Meditations* 2. 9.

15. Descartes, *Treatise on Man* 11. 120.

16. Gilbert Ryle, *The Concept of Mind* (New York, 1949), p. 15.

17. LeRoy Moore, "From Profane to Sacred America," *Journal of the American Academy of Religion*, Vol. 34 (Sept. 1971), p. 337.

18. Friedrich Nietzsche, *Beyond Good and Evil*, Preface.

19. Friedrich Nietzsche, *The Antichrist* 14.

20. Friedrich Nietzsche, *The Will to Power* 2. 227.

21. Sam Keen and Anne Fox, *Telling Your Story* (New York, 1973), p. 20.

22. W. D. Davies, *Christian Origins and Judaism* (Philadelphia, 1962), p. 1; cf. Donald M. Baillie, *God Was in Christ* (New York, 1948), p. 10.

23. Strommen *et al.*, *A Study of Generations*, pp. 117, 367.

24. E.g., Charles Y. Glock and Rodney Stark, *Religion and Society in Tension* (Chicago, 1965), p. 95.

25. John Knox, *The Death of Christ* (New York, 1958), p. 70.

26. Sam Keen, *To a Dancing God* (New York, 1970), pp. 144, 159, 160.

27. Cf. Bonaventura, *Life of St. Francis* 5. 4.

28. *Minutes of the General Assembly of the United Presbyterian Church in the U.S.A.* (Philadelphia, 1970), Vol. I, p. 897.

29. Keen, *To a Dancing God*, p. 143.

30. Cf. Alan Walker, "Where Pentecostalism Is Mushrooming," *The Christian Century*, Vol. 85 (Jan. 17, 1968), p. 81.

31. *Nephesh* is poorly rendered as "soul" in the King James and Revised Standard versions.

Index

BIBLICAL TEXTS

NAMES AND SUBJECTS

Abelard, Peter, 54, 64
Abraham, 69, 113, 142
Agapē, 16, 64, 98–110, 154, 159, 161
Allegorical interpretation, 31–32, 48–66
Ambrose, bishop, 31–32, 53, 59, 122
Anthony, monk, 118, 120
Aquinas, Thomas, 56, 70, 111, 148
Aristotle, 76, 78, 105, 107, 127, 136
Asceticism, 49, 52, 55, 59, 62, 74, 112, 119, 135, 145, 148, 154
Auden, W. H., 96
Augustine of Hippo, 32–33, 54, 86, 107, 109, 111, 120, 122, 147–148

Baldwin, James, 128
Baptism, 14, 86, 90–91
Basil, bishop, 68, 155
Bernard of Clairvaux, 53–56, 63–64
Blake, William, 70, 72
Bonhoeffer, Dietrich, 65–66
Brown, Norman, 13
Browning, Robert, 46
Brunner, Emil, 75
Bunyan, John, 36

Callahan, Sidney, 80, 90
Calvin, John, 9, 35, 59–60, 119–121, 125–126
Carter, Sydney, 41
Castellio, Sebastian, 60
Catholicism, Roman, 40, 42, 56–57, 85, 88, 95, 96, 136, 138, 156
Chardin, Pierre Teilhard de, 126
Christology, 16, 94, 157, 158
Chrysostom, John, 29, 68, 134
Cicero, 30, 31, 38
Clement of Alexandria, 28, 131, 134
Cox, Harvey, 27, 138
Creation, Genesis accounts of, 13, 46, 112, 113, 132, 140, 141

Dante Alighieri, 56, 108–109
David, King of Israel, 19, 21, 25, 29,

34, 35, 37, 100, 113, 116, 130
Davies, Mary Carolyn, 77
Descartes, René, 156
Dickinson, Emily, 109
Docetism, 131, 157–158
Donne, John, 132
Dostoevsky, Fyodor, 131
Dualism, mind-body, 11–15, 65, 154–157

Eliade, Mircea, 150
Ellis, Havelock, 88, 153
Encounter groups, 13, 128–129, 159
Eucharist, 53, 84–92, 95, 117, 121–122, 133

Fall of man, 54, 161
Fra Angelico, 153
Francis of Assisi, 120, 161
Freud, Sigmund, 67, 74–75, 157

Gibran, Kahlil, 124
Gnosticism, 51, 82
Goethe, J. W. von, 61, 92
Gregory of Nyssa, 28, 52–53

Herder, J. G. von, 61
Hillel, 115
Hinduism, 17, 82
Holism, 14–15, 40, 43, 46, 71, 146, 158–159

Incarnation, 13, 16, 159
Islam, 21, 55, 145–147, 150, 151

Jerome, 52, 59, 118–120
Jesus, 11, 24–26, 31, 41, 50, 51, 66, 67–83, 86–89, 92–94, 102–106, 109, 117–118, 121–122, 124, 125, 131–132, 137, 138, 142–144, 154, 157–158
Josephus, 47, 139
Jovinian, 58–59

Khayyám, Omar, 147
Keen, Sam, 156, 158–159, 162